# SANTA BARBARA
## *Cooks!*

# SANTA BARBARA
# *Cooks!*

*Original recipes from*
*Santa Barbara's best restaurants*

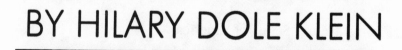

# BY HILARY DOLE KLEIN

## CONARI PRESS
## BERKELEY, CALIFORNIA

Printed in the United States of America

Cover design and illustration by Joan Edwards

ISBN: 0-943233-02-X

For Milton and Ruth
With love and gratitude

# Table of Contents

# *Introduction*

When I was growing up in Santa Barbara, with six brothers and sisters, eating out at a restaurant was a truly rare event. I can count on my fingers those special occasions when we went out, and they had to put several tables together to accommodate us.

My most magical memories are of a Chinese restaurant on Lower State Street. We ate in a dining room upstairs, and the food came up from the kitchens on wonderful creaking dumb waiters. The restaurant was totally exotic to me, brightly decorated in red, green and gold, with rushing waiters with impenetrable accents. I remember my parents' pleasure at the prices, and walking back to the car, eating my chocolate covered mint, sorry that the dinner was over.

When my grandparents came to Santa Barbara in the winters, my grandmother took me on special occasions to the Copper Coffee Pot for lunch, and I would push my tray through the line, amazed at all the tempting choices I could make. But I always ordered the chicken pie.

And then there was a diner on Upper State Street where we went occasionally because they had, as my father told me very seriously, "the best hamburgers in town." Even then I had the notion that one of the purposes of life was to discover the best dish in town, and honor the place by returning to order it.

I was lucky to marry someone who likes to eat out as much as I do and our children learned early that our most pleasant dinners as a family seem to take place in restaurants. So when I was asked to write the weekly "Hot Spots" restaurant column for the *Santa Barbara News-Press*, it was a fortuitous mix of business and pleasure. In turn, writing "Hot Spots" gave me the familiarity with Santa Barbara's restaurants that enabled me to put this book together.

I can remember when it seemed as if Santa Barbara turned off the lights and rolled up the sidewalks shortly after seven p.m., and a good restaurant was one that poured a lot of drinks. Over the years, I have seen our restaurants getting better and better. Santa Barbara has gone from a sleepy, backwater place with ordinary restaurants, to a very cosmopolitan town with sophisticated tastes. Here on California's Riviera, we can truly brag about "Santa Barbara cuisine." It is characterized by its ethnic diversity, an abundance of fish, a reliance on fresh ingredients, glorious sauces, and very imaginative chefs. We are fortunate indeed that a small town like ours can support so many interesting restaurants, and with this book you can now cook at home the dishes that people from all over the world have tasted and admired.

Working with the chefs and restaurateurs to collect these recipes has shown me a different side of the restaurant business than sitting down, ordering, and having a good time. Chefs are incredibly busy people. If they're not in the kitchen, they're on the phone with their distributors, or working on their accounts. Pinning down some of these men and women has been harder than catching fireflies at noon.

Still, it's been a pleasure to get into their kitchens. I have smelled heavenly osso bucco in the tiny kitchen at the Wine Cask, seen Norbert Schulz swiftly measure out the ingredients for a pastry at Norbert's, watched Jerry Wilson pulling bones out of a great salmon at Oysters, accompanied Marc Ehrler as he inspected his smoker at the San Ysidro Ranch, and interrupted Nancy Weiss putting together a salad at Soho. Visiting the restaurants kept me in a constant state of hunger at the thought of all the good food about to be served.

As the recipes came in from all over Santa Barbara, the book began to take on a personality of its own. What I like about it is its variety and diversity. It contains recipes from the Caribbean to Catalonia, from Northern Africa to Peru, and from Greece to Thailand. They range from the very simple Chicken Corn Soup from Hibachi to the elaborate Sablé Heart's Desire from Michael's Waterside. I am especially pleased with the remarkable sauces to be found here, sauces as refreshing as The Chalkboard's Papaya, Mint, and Green Chile Salsa, as savory as Red Onion Marmalade from Four Seasons Biltmore, and as tasty as Downey's Apricot Champagne Sauce.

All of the recipes in the book have been adapted slightly for home use. I hope that it will make choosing where to go out to eat more fun, and cooking at home more interesting.

I would like to thank Teddy, who hates my cooking and is always ready to eat out; and John, my constant companion, whose lines are worth stealing; and his parents with whom we've had so many great meals. I would also like to thank Annette Burden and Lisa Merkl for their invaluable help when I needed it most.

### Banana Reef
### 514 State Street, Santa Barbara
### 564-8511

When my family took me out to dinner on Mother's Day in Fort Benton, Montana in 1981, we dished up turkey and mashed potatoes from steam tables set up in the middle of the restaurant. I was the only woman in the room not wearing a corsage on polyester. "Just you wait," said a voice in my heart. "One day you'll live in a town that can give you tastes from France and Mexico, flavors from Thailand and India, samplings from Italy and Peru. Even, glory of glories, food from the Caribbean." And now I do.

Banana Reef is a million years from Fort Benton. The Caribbean restaurant sashayed into an enticing, palm-filled setting on Lower State Street recently, bringing with it a colorful ambience and a good sense of fun. There's a big red parrot (alive) in the patio and a much bigger shark's head (mounted) over the Island-style bar. Bright red chairs and colorful Caribbean art decorate the dining-room, the big outdoor patio is covered with a striped canopy, and steel drum music (live on Thursdays) pulsates through the air. People literally dance to their seats.

I love this kind of food. It's all slightly familiar, yet exotic and new. Caribbean cooking draws from a variety of influences: French, Spanish, South American, Dutch, Cuban, and Indian among them. Instead of ketchup and mustard on the table, there's Island Heat pepper sauce and Jamaican Jerk, a sweet dipping sauce. Jerk is a common Caribbean seasoning, tangy and spicy, and Banana Reef has their's made-to-order in Miami. The menu features such Island classics as Miami Beef and Mango, Lime Garlic Shrimp, and Kingston Curried Chicken.

My constant companion summed it up: "This place is like a vacation." He took another bite of Sweet Potatoes and Cream. "The only problem is, how do we cook it ourselves? We just haven't evolved that far." Not true. Here are a few recipes to prove him wrong.

## MA CHANCES CHICKEN SALAD

**4 whole boneless chicken breasts**
**1 tablespoon curry powder**
**1 cup curried mayonnaise (recipe follows)**
**½ cup celery, chopped**
**¼ cup golden raisins**
**2 tablespoons toasted coconut**
**¼ cup cashews**
**salt and pepper to taste**

Coat the chicken with the curry powder and bake it in a foil-covered pan in a 375 degree oven for 20 minutes. Chill and then cut into small pieces. Mix the chicken with the rest of the ingredients and let stand for 1 hour. Serves 6.

## *Curried Mayonnaise*

**1 cup mayonnaise**
**1 tablespoon lemon juice**
**1 teaspoon curry powder**

Combine ingredients. Makes 1 cup.

# SWEET POTATOES AND CREAM

**4 medium-sized sweet potatoes**
**1 teaspoon butter**
**½ cup cubed Edam cheese, about ½ pound**
**1 cup heavy cream**
**salt and pepper to taste**
**ground nutmeg to taste**

Peel the sweet potatoes and slice them thinly. Coat an 8-inch square baking pan with butter, and spread a layer of the potatoes on the bottom. Sprinkle ¼ of the cheese on top, and pour on ¼ of the cream. Season with salt, pepper, and ground nutmeg. Repeat the process until all ingredients are used. Cover with foil and bake at 350 degrees for 1 hour, or until the potatoes are cooked. Serves 6.

# MIAMI BEEF AND MANGO

**3 fresh mangoes**
**12 beef fillet medallions, 4 ounces each**
**½ cup flour**
**3 tablespoons butter**
**1 cup champagne**
**2 cups heavy cream**
**salt and pepper**

Peel and trim the mangoes. Puree ½ of them and slice the other half and save.

Trim the medallions. Dredge each one in flour, and set aside. Heat the butter in a skillet large enough to hold all the meat. Add the fillets and cook over medium high heat, approximately 5 minutes per side for medium rare. Remove from the pan and keep warm.

Add the champagne and stir to de-glaze the pan. Cook until the liquid is reduced by half. Lower heat, and add the heavy cream. Add the pureed mangoes, and season with salt and pepper. Cook until just heated through. Pour sauce onto serving platter and place the medallions on the sauce. Top with the sliced mangoes. Serves 6.

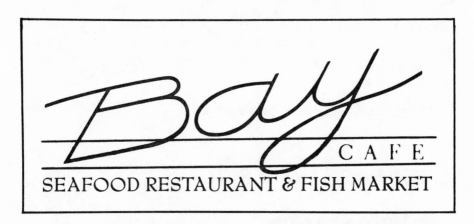

## Bay Cafe Seafood Restaurant and Fish Market
### 131 Anacapa Street, Santa Barbara
### 963-2215

Located on Anacapa Street between the ocean and the freeway, the Bay Cafe is a little off the beaten path, but it's well worth finding. In fact, it was voted the best seafood restaurant in a poll of 52 of the area's top chefs and restaurant owners.

Bay Cafe has lots of grey tiles, high tech chairs, white tablecloths, and lovely prints on the walls. The acoustics make it one of the most pleasant and relaxing restaurants in town for good conversation. It also has seating outdoors in a pretty patio.

Known for its fresh fish with great sauces and unique pasta dishes, the Bay Cafe uses only local fish. The fresh catch of the day is up on the board, but if you really want to see what looks good you can wander over to the fish market and get an idea of what to order by admiring the fresh fish in the big glass cases.

Owners Bryn and Larry Martin change the menu every six to eight months, incorporating the specials that have really hit it off, like the Roma Ravioli, Swordfish Flambe and Santa Barbara Ceviche I've included here. A lot of people think that ceviche is raw fish. Actually it's cooked without heat or flame. The reaction with the lime juice and salt cooks the fish. But, as Larry Martin points out, it is very important to start with really fresh fish to make good ceviche. Their version is great for a warm Santa Barbara afternoon or dinner.

Larry described Bay Cafe's food as Santa Barbara cuisine, which he says means a combination of California, Mexican and French influences. A winning combination, as the other chefs in town also have attested to.

# *SANTA BARBARA CEVICHE*

**1 pound halibut, very fresh**
**1 pound king salmon, very fresh**
**½ pound fresh bay scallops**
**7-10 limes**
**2 tomatoes, diced**
**2 sticks celery, diced**
**1 sweet red onion, sliced extra thin in rings**
**½ bunch cilantro, chopped**
**1-4 jalapenos, diced (Use 1-2 for medium hot "gringo" or 3-4**
**for hot "macho")**
**1 ounce fresh garlic, chopped and blended with a little olive**
**oil**
**salt and ground white pepper to taste**

Check the fish for bones and remove. Cut the fillets into paper thin slices. Squeeze the limes, removing any seeds. Combine the fish, vegetables, and herbs together with the lime juice in a large glass bowl and gently toss together. Add salt and pepper to taste. Refrigerate for at least 1 hour. Serve on small, chilled plates. Serves 6-8 as an appetizer.

# ROMA RAVIOLI

2 ounces olive oil
8-10 fresh Roma tomatoes
2 sprigs parsley, chopped
6 cloves garlic, peeled and diced
1 bell pepper, chopped
1 red onion, sliced
4 mushrooms, sliced
2 pinches dried oregano
1 pinch fennel seed
½ cup red wine, preferably Cabernet
½ cup water
20 cheese ravioli
1 cup heavy cream
¼ pound sweet butter
salt and coarse black pepper to taste
16 jumbo prawns, peeled and deveined
grated fresh Parmesan cheese

Heat the olive oil in a large skillet. Add all the vegetables and herbs. Saute over medium heat until cooked, but still crisp. Add the wine and water, and cook for 5 minutes over medium heat to reduce.

While the sauce is reducing, cook the ravioli in boiling salted water until they are al dente, about 10-15 minutes. Drain, toss with a dash of olive oil, cover, and keep warm.

Pour the sauce into a food processor or blender and puree. Return to the pan and add the heavy cream. As it heats up, whisk in the butter. If the sauce is a little too thick at this point, add a touch of water. Add salt and pepper to taste. Add the shrimp to the tomato sauce and, keeping the flame low, cook the shrimp for about 3-4 minutes.

Place 5 ravioli on each plate, cover with sauce, and circle with 4 shrimp per plate. Top with fresh grated Parmesan cheese. Serves 4.

# SWORDFISH FLAMBE

**4 fresh swordfish steaks (8 ounces each)**
**½ cup flour**
**seasoned salt to taste**
**4 ounces clarified butter**
**10 mushrooms, sliced**
**¼ pound sweet butter**
**1 pinch of dried thyme**
**¾ cup dry white wine**
**¼ cup brandy**
**½ cup heavy cream**
**salt and coarse black pepper to taste**
**1 small can pimientos**

Preheat the oven to 375 degrees. Dip the swordfish steaks in flour and lightly season on one side with seasoned salt. In a large saute pan, heat the clarified butter. When hot, place the fish in the pan and brown on one side, then turn over. Add the mushrooms, sweet butter, thyme, and white wine. Add the brandy and tip the pan into the burner so that it catches the liquid and begins to flame (flambe). Cook for about 2 minutes. Remove the fish and place in the oven at 375 degrees for 3-4 minutes to finish cooking.

Meanwhile, add the cream to the saute pan and reduce it until you have a nice creamy sauce. Pour the sauce onto 4 dinner plates and gently place the fish on top. Garnish by topping the swordfish with red pimientos. Serve with rice pilaf and fresh, steamed vegetables. Serves 4.

# TIGER SAUTE

**1 ounce olive oil**
**1 red bell pepper, sliced**
**1 green pepper, sliced**
**10 mushrooms, sliced**
**2 tomatoes, diced**
**1½ pounds Tiger shrimp, cleaned and deveined**
**3 garlic cloves, crushed**
**3 ounces sweet butter**
**1 pinch dried thyme**
**½ cup white wine, preferably Sauvignon Blanc**
**½ cup clam juice**
**salt and ground white pepper to taste**

In a large saute pan, heat the olive oil over high heat. When hot, add the red pepper, green pepper, mushrooms, and tomatoes. Saute over high heat for 2-3 minutes. Then add the Tiger shrimp, garlic, butter, thyme, wine, and clam juice. Cook for about 3-4 more minutes or until shrimp are cooked through. Add salt and white pepper. Serves 6.

## Brigitte's
## 1327 State Street, Santa Barbara
## 966-9676

I almost hate to spread the word. Brigitte's is a romantic little gem of a restaurant, modestly tucked into a narrow space on State Street, a few doors up from the Arlington Theater. And now that you know where it is, you may as well pronounce it right: Bri-ghee'tas.

The first time I ate there, I thought I had died and gone to heaven. This was several years ago, right after moving here from Great Falls, Montana. In Great Falls, an exciting restaurant is one that serves a combination of Chinese, Italian and American cuisine—without the aid of a single vegetable.

But even now that I have become accustomed to the freshest of fish and find myself blase about the babiest of vegetables, Brigitte's is still a great treat. Long and narrow, and very intimate, the restaurant comfortably juggles formality and casualness. Linen napkins grace the tables, while stacks of wine boxes line the walls. The long wooden bar that separates the two small dining areas is a good place to wait for a table.

Brigitte Guehr and her husband, Norbert Schulz, also own Norbert's. At Brigitte's no reservations are accepted, so it's strictly first come first serve. The menu, like the list of daily specials, is short, with just a few selections each of salad, appetizers, pizza, pasta, and entrees from the grill. But the dishes are so highly imaginative, that it's hard to choose from even a few.

Try picking between a warm Spinach Salad with Spicy Fried Oysters and Hot Sausage Shallot Dressing or an Arugula and Watercress Salad with Apple, Almonds, and Fried Brie. And how do you choose between the two entrees featured here: Tomato Linguini with Chicken and Ginger, and Grilled Mahi Mahi with Toasted Macadamia Nut Butter and Grilled Pineapple Relish?

You just have to go with friends who don't mind your fork in their plates. And it all tastes as good as it sounds.

# BUTTERNUT SQUASH CURRY SOUP WITH TOASTED ALMONDS OR SUNFLOWER SEEDS

**4 ounces butter**
**1 pound butternut squash, peeled and diced finely**
**1 onion, diced**
**4-6 tablespoons curry powder**
**1 quart good chicken stock**
**1 cup heavy cream**
**salt and cayenne to taste**
**sugar or coconut milk to taste**
**1 handful toasted almonds or sunflower seeds**

Melt the butter in a large saucepan. Add the squash and onion, and saute over medium high heat for about 5 minutes. Add the curry, and saute again for about 1 minute. Add chicken stock to this mixture and simmer, uncovered, for 10 minutes. Puree the soup in a blender. Put back in the pan, add the cream, and heat over low heat again. Add salt, cayenne, and a little sugar or coconut milk to taste. Sprinkle with almonds or sunflower seeds. Serves 6.

# TOMATO LINGUINI
# WITH CHICKEN AND GINGER

**1 pound tomato pasta, fresh or dried**
**4 tablespoons olive oil, plus a little more**
**3 whole boneless chicken breasts, skinned and sliced into**
     **strips ½ inch thick**
**½ ounce chopped ginger**
**½ ounce chopped cilantro, plus a few sprigs for garnish**
**½ cup chopped fresh tomato, peeled and seeded**
**½ cup fresh Anaheim chilies, roasted, peeled and seeded (or**
     **used canned)**
**1/3 cup pine nuts**
**salt and cayenne pepper to taste**

Bring to a boil 3 quarts of water to which a little olive oil has
been added. Add the pasta and cook until al dente (2 minutes if
fresh).

Meanwhile, in a large skillet, heat 2 tablespoons olive oil over
medium high heat. Add the chicken and saute until just cooked
through. Add the ginger, cilantro, tomato, chilies and pine nuts.
Stir. Drain the pasta and add it to the chicken. Add the remaining 2 tablespoons of olive oil, season with salt and cayenne
pepper, and toss. Divide on plates and garnish with fresh cilantro. Serves 6.

# GRILLED MAHI MAHI WITH TOASTED MACADAMIA NUT BUTTER AND GRILLED PINEAPPLE RELISH

**6 mahi mahi (5-6 ounces each)**
**juice from 2 limes**
**salt to taste**
**¾ cup Toasted Macadamia Nut Butter (recipe follows)**
**Grilled Pineapple Relish (recipe follows)**

Season the mahi mahi with lime juice and salt. Over a barbecue, a grill, or in the broiler, grill until cooked to your preference. Place the Macadamia Butter on a plate, then place the fish on top. Serve the Pineapple Relish on top of the fish or on the side. Serves 6.

## Toasted Macadamia Nut Butter

**6 ounces macadamia nuts, finely chopped**
**4 ounces butter**

Place nuts and butter in a small pan and cook over medium low until both are well browned. Makes ¾ cup.

## Grilled Pineapple Relish

**6 small slices pineapple**
**¼ cup orange juice**
**¼ cup lime juice**
**1 ounce cilantro, chopped**
**1 small jalapeno, diced**
**½ an orange and lime, peeled and diced**

Grill the pineapple slices over a barbecue, a grill, or in the broiler, about 3-4 minutes a side. When cool, dice them finely. Mix well with the rest of the ingredients. Makes about 2 cups.

## Brophy Bros. Clam Bar and Restaurant
## 119 Harbor Way, Santa Barbara
## 966-4418

With the smells of salt water, fish, and boat engines, the sounds of sea gulls and hulls slapping against the water, and the sight of hundreds of boats, a trip to the harbor is like stepping into a picture puzzle. Brophy Bros. is right in the middle of the picture. The restaurant is up on the second floor, and big windows, as well as a wrap-around balcony, maximize the view that always makes me want to get out a set of oil paintings.

If I were working as a waitress again, I think I'd like to work at Brophy Bros. If people don't come for the scenery, they come for the fresh, fresh fish, and the very popular bar—and they come in droves. Even in the sleepy mid-afternoons, the place is filled. The waiters and waitresses really get a good work out, and their customers are always happy.

The restaurant is a perfect stop off for people who have been working on the boats all day, and for those who wish they had. The red tablecloth covered tables are shoved close together, the ceilings are low, the floors are wood, and the walls are filled with nautical photographs.

They serve one of the best chowders in Santa Barbara and they have vats of fresh oysters on ice behind the bar. The basic menu is fairly simple: clams, ceviche, mussels, seafood salads, and fried fish. There are also daily specials. The fish is as fresh as it gets, so the specials change constantly, and the sauces are quirky and interesting. I especially like the Tuna with Cashews and Shallot Tarragon Mustard included here.

Billy Molloy, who recently switched from head chef to restaurant manager, gave me these recipes. It must have been much more predictable dealing with the changing catches of fish than it is dealing with the endless streams of customers and crises at this busy establishment. But he looks like he's thriving on it.

# FRESH AHI TUNA WITH CASHEWS AND SHALLOT TARRAGON MUSTARD SAUCE

**3 ounces cashews**
**3 ounces bread crumbs**
**1 egg, beaten**
**½ cup water**
**4 tuna steaks, 1/3-½ pound each**
**¼ cup peanut oil**
**Shallot Tarragon Mustard Sauce (recipe follows)**

Chop the cashews, and mix them together with the bread crumbs. Mix the water and egg together in a bowl large enough to fit the fish. Dip the tuna into this mixture and then roll the egg-coated tuna in the crumbs, pressing them into the fish with your hands.

Heat the peanut oil in a large skillet, and saute the fish over medium high heat for approximately 10 minutes per inch thickness of fish. Serve the fish with sauce on the top or on the side. Serves 4.

## Shallot Tarragon Mustard Sauce

**2 tablespoons butter**
**2 tablespoons shallots, finely diced**
**½ cup wine**
**3 teaspoons Dijon mustard**
**1 teaspoon tarragon**
**½ cup cream**
**salt and pepper to taste**

Melt the butter in a pan, add the shallots, and cook for 3 minutes on low heat. Add the wine, mustard, and tarragon, and simmer until reduced by half. Add the cream, stirring constantly. Cook 2 minutes, then add salt and pepper to taste.

# MAHI MAHI WITH LIME AND CRACKED BLACK PEPPER BEURRE BLANC

**Cracked Black Pepper Beurre Blanc (recipe follows)**
**4 mahi mahi fillets**

Make the Beurre Blanc. Broil or saute the mahi mahi fillets for approximately 3-4 minutes on each side. Serve with the sauce. Serves 4.

## Cracked Black Pepper Beurre Blanc

**1 teaspoon cracked black pepper**
**¼ cup finely diced shallots**
**¼ cup vermouth**
**¼ cup lemon juice**
**juice of 1 lime**
**½ pound unsalted butter, cut into pieces of 1 ounce or less**

In a non-aluminum sauce pan, combine the cracked black pepper, shallots, vermouth, lemon juice, and lime juice. Reduce until nearly dry, but be careful not to scorch.

Remove the pan from the heat. Add 1-2 pieces of butter, and stir until the butter is melted. Return the pan to the heat, and continue adding the butter, 1 piece at a time, on low heat. If the butter separates, the heat is too high. In that case, remove the pan from the heat, and whisk rapidly to re-emulsify.

The sauce can be kept until ready to serve in a double boiler over barely simmering water. Makes about 1 cup.

## Cafe Picasso
## 18 West Figueroa Street, Santa Barbara
## 962-6265

Cafe Picasso is one of the smallest restaurants in Santa Barbara, but it's small like a Faberge egg. Once inside, you are enveloped in a cocoon of soft peach and all the details are exquisite, from the elegant black chairs to the lovely silver and glasses.

The restaurant has less than a dozen tables, with additional seating on stools at a bar overlooking the open kitchen. The kitchen is the envy of Santa Barbara cooks, with its rows of gleaming copper pans, its brass and stainless steel range hood, and beautiful etched glass.

Situated on a side street, just off of State Street, the restaurant brings to Santa Barbara Middle Eastern food wedded to classic French cooking. Cafe Picasso features wonderful appetizers like hummus and pastilla, which is layers of pastry with Cornish hen, lemon, onions, saffron, and eggs, sprinkled with cinnamon and sugar. And the Baba Ghannouj, an eggplant appetizer, is worth a trip to the restaurant (or you can make it at home following the recipe here).

Cafe Picasso is owned by Youssef Fakhouri, who used to be a chef at the Casa Madrona in Sausalito. He brought in his brother, Abraham, who is a classically trained five-star chef, to cook. The entrees they serve are a mixture of French dishes, like the Escalope de Veau au Poivre, and traditional North African dishes, like couscous. You can order the couscous with chicken, lamb, or vegetarian style, but the Couscous Royale described here is the best in my opinion. Youssef explained that the French recipes came from his brother, while he himself contributed the Couscous Royale and the Baba Ghannouj.

Cafe Picasso proves that good things come in small packages.

# BABA GHANNOUJ (EGGPLANT APPETIZER)

**2 eggplants, each weighing 1 pound**
**1 cup sesame tahini**
**1 cup plain yogurt**
**2 large cloves garlic, minced**
**1 teaspoon salt**
**freshly ground black pepper to taste**
**1/3-½ cup lemon juice, to taste**
**2 tablespoons toasted sesame seeds**
**1 pinch paprika**
**2 tablespoons olive oil**
**1 package pita bread**

If using a gas stove, grill the eggplants over a low flame, turning them slowly until they soften and begin to collapse, and the skin is crisp and charred. Remove and cool.

If using an electric stove, place the eggplants on a baking sheet, 5-6 inches under the broiler. Broil with the oven door ajar for 15-20 minutes, turning frequently, until the eggplants collapse and are evenly charred. Remove and cool.

When the eggplants are cool, cut off the charred skin. Place the skinless eggplant into a blender or food processor. Add the tahini, yogurt, garlic, salt, pepper, and lemon juice to taste. Puree until a smooth, fairly firm dip results.

Transfer to a serving dish and chill well. Garnish with sesame seeds, paprika, and olive oil. Serve with pita bread cut into wedges for dipping. Serves 8.

# COUSCOUS ROYAL

2 medium Cornish game hens, cut in half
1 bay leaf
1 teaspoon cinnamon
2 teaspoons salt
¼ teaspoon black pepper
2½-3 cups water
6 medium carrots, cut into 2 inch lengths
6 turnips, cut into quarters
1 pound pumpkin, peeled and cut into 1-inch chunks
4 small zucchini, cut into 2-inch lengths
3 medium onions, chopped
1 tablespoon butter
1 teaspoon caraway seeds, crushed
1½ cups cooked garbanzo beans
2 ounces raisins
1 pinch saffron
1 pound rack of lamb, cut into chops
1 package couscous
1 bunch parsley, chopped
1 small can of harissa sauce, optional (available at Middle East
   markets)

Place the Cornish game hen halves in a large pot with the bay
leaf, cinnamon, salt, and pepper. Add enough water to cover the
hens, bring to a boil, and simmer, partially covered, for 40
minutes.

Add the carrots, turnips, pumpkin, and zucchini. Add more
water, if necessary, to cover the vegetables. Bring to a boil, and
simmer for an additional 20 minutes, partially covered.

Meanwhile, lightly saute the onions in butter. Add the crushed
caraway seeds, garbanzo beans, raisins, and saffron. Cook on
low heat for 10-15 minutes. Set aside.

Season the lamb chops with salt and pepper, and cook in a
frying pan until well done, about 10 minutes per side.

Prepare the couscous according to package directions. When ready, place hot, buttered couscous on a large serving platter, making a well in the center. Arrange the Cornish hens and vegetables in the center of the well. Place the lamb chops around the edges of the dish. Cover with the onion mixture, and sprinkle with chopped parsley. Use the broth from the hens and vegetables as gravy, adding harissa sauce, if desired. Serves 6-8.

# *POULET AUX OLIVES ET CITRONS (CHICKEN WITH OLIVES AND LEMON)*

**1 cup olive oil**
**1 teaspoon ginger**
**½ package saffron**
**1 teaspoon crushed coriander seeds**
**1 teaspoon salt (or to taste)**
**1 4-ounce jar green olives, drained**
**1 quart water**
**3 medium onions, chopped**
**4 garlic cloves, crushed**
**4 medium Cornish game hens, cut in half**
**parsley for garnish**
**2 pickled lemons, sliced (or use regular lemons)**

Preheat the oven to 350 degrees. Mix the oil, ginger, saffron, coriander, salt, olives, water, onions, and garlic in a pot. Cook, partially covered, over medium heat for 20-30 minutes. Sauce should have a nice smooth consistency; reduce if necessary.

Put the Cornish hens in a large baking dish, and pour the sauce over. Bake, uncovered, at 350 degrees for 40-50 minutes. Garnish with parsley and slices of lemon. Serves 4-6.

# ESCALOPE DE VEAU AU POIVRE (PEPPER VEAL)

**4 tablespoons butter**
**8 slices veal scallopine, 2 ounces each**
**3 tablespoons minced onions**
**½ teaspoon minced garlic**
**¼ cup chopped mushrooms**
**½ cup veal stock (or substitute chicken or beef broth)**
**1 cup heavy cream**
**1 tablespoon Dijon mustard**
**2 teaspoons green peppercorns**
**salt to taste, optional**

Melt the butter over high heat in a large, heavy frying pan.
Quickly saute the veal scallopine, 4 at a time, until golden
brown. Remove from the pan, and keep warm.

Add the onions, garlic, and mushrooms to the pan. Saute 2-3
minutes, until light brown. Add the stock and cream. Reduce
heat and simmer, until the sauce begins to thicken—don't let the
cream curdle. Add the mustard, peppercorns, and salt if desired.
Pour the sauce over the veal. This goes nicely with rice.
Serves 4.

## Cafe Vallarta
## 626 East Haley Street, Santa Barbara
## 564-8494

Cafe Vallarta is almost hidden beside the more famous La Tolteca Tortilla Factory on Haley Street. But once you find it, this restaurant is pleasant indeed and the food is quite good.

Freshly white-washed, with brightly painted blue beams and trim, it has been cheerfully decorated with painted tiles, woven baskets and garlands of vegetables. I imagine it could just as easily be a cafe in Puerta Vallarta, the sister city for whom it was named.

The first night we ate there, the cook hadn't shown up. This was no problem, however, because the owner, Justo Gracia, had taken over in the kitchen, preparing the dishes he developed in the first place. His parents had owned a restaurant when he was a child, and, in Cafe Vallarta, he finally has realized the dream of starting one of his own. He calls his food "the authentic, popular way of eating in Mexico."

At Cafe Vallarta, a simple taco is a delight: the meat is superb, the tortilla freshly made, and it comes with sweet, mild, shredded cabbage instead of lettuce. I've eaten enchiladas with rice and beans for years. But at Cafe Vallarta, this is a whole new meal. The beans (black beans from Yucatan) are succulent, the rice (with potatoes and onions) delicate, and the chicken enchilada delicious.

The cafe boasts a large menu, with unique tostadas, burritos, enchiladas and tacos. There are also a number of specialties, seafood and antojitos ("little whims"). The Chicken in Mole Poblano included here is terrific, with a sweet, dark but delicate sauce. Gracia says it is typical of the simplicity of his cooking.

Ten kinds of coffee (they serve breakfast too) make this a true cafe. The reasonable prices make it a very good find. The live music at night turns this place into a party. But the food is the best part of all.

## HUEVOS RANCHEROS

**2 teaspoons butter (or corn oil)**
**1 corn tortilla**
**2 eggs**
**Salsa (recipe follows)**
**hot sauce, optional**

In a small frying pan, melt 1 teaspoon of the butter (or heat the oil) over medium heat, and cook the corn tortilla until it is soft. Remove the tortilla to a plate and keep warm. In the same pan, heat the remaining butter or oil and cook 2 eggs over easy.
Place the eggs on the tortilla. Pour the salsa on top of the eggs. For extra flavor, add a little hot sauce. Serves 1.

## Salsa

**1 ripe tomato**
**½ onion, diced**
**½ serrano chile, diced**
**1 sprig cilantro, chopped**
**2 fresh mushrooms, sliced**
**salt to taste**

Place all the ingredients in a small pan, and cook them just long enough to heat. Stir constantly to avoid sticking. Add salt to taste. Makes 2 servings.

# YUCATAN BLACK BEANS

**1 pound dried black beans**
**6 cups water**
**2 tablespoons corn oil**
**1 small Spanish onion, chopped**
**salt and lemon pepper to taste**

Wash the beans well. In a deep pot with a lid, bring the beans and water to a boil, lower heat and simmer, covered, for 1½-2 hours, or until the beans are soft. In a separate pan, heat the oil and cook the Spanish onion until limp. Add the onion to the beans, along with salt and lemon pepper, and cook for another 10 minutes. Serves 4-6.

# CHICKEN IN MOLE POBLANO SAUCE

**2 tablespoons oil**
**1 3-pound chicken, cut into 8 pieces**
**5 cups water**
**5 fresh mushrooms, sliced**
**1 carrot, chopped**
**6 pacilla chilies, dried**
**2 cans mole poblano, La Victoria brand**

In a large frying pan, heat the oil and then brown the chicken over high heat until golden on all sides. Remove from heat.

In a large pot with a lid, place 4-5 teaspoons of the chicken drippings and 4 cups of the water. Add the mushrooms and carrot; bring to a boil, then cover, lower heat, and simmer for about 6 minutes.

While stock is simmering, remove the seeds from the pacilla chilies and put the chilies in a blender with the remaining cup of water. Blend until the mixture becomes well colored. Strain this liquid, and add it to the liquid in the pot. Add the mole poblano and the chicken pieces. Cook on medium heat, for 15-20 minutes or until chicken is cooked through, stirring occasionally. If sauce looks too thick, add more water. Serves 5-6.

## Cajun Kitchen
### 1924 De La Vina Street, Santa Barbara
### 687-2062

When I go out for breakfast, what I like is a place that's casual and cozy enough to allow the waking up process to go on in comfort. But I also want a place that's special, that can sustain that early morning feeling of promise. For years, the Cajun Kitchen has been my kind of breakfast place. Recently they began to serve dinners too, so now their reliable brand of warm service keeps going all day long. And so does the authentic Cajun cooking, which is served along with a number of Mexican and American dishes.

The first time I went there, I ordered grits. I had been reading about them for years and was delighted to have a chance to try them. I thought they were going to be spicy, oniony and crunchy. Boy, was I surprised when they turned out more like Cream of Wheat. I now order the Jambalaya with Louisiana Hot Sausage, Shrimp, Ham, and Chicken and a couple of eggs on top instead. The Cajun Kitchen is the most creative place in town when it comes to designing your own breakfast. You can have your eggs with seven kinds of sausages and meats. Then pick between home fries, hash browns or grits, and select from toast, English muffins, flour tortillas, homemade biscuits, muffins or corn bread. They serve 14 omelettes, as well as specials, pancakes, and French toast.

With its hanging macrame planters, dried flower bouquets, and shingled walls, The Cajun Kitchen has something of a pleasant sixties' feeling. And for those who like the warmth of the sun, it has a walled, sunny patio out in front. It's just as pleasant and cozy at night as it is during the day. Owner/chef Richard Jimenez' menu of Cajun cooking features such dishes as seafood gumbo, jambalaya, Cajun country steak, red beans and rice, and several kinds of blackened fish. He developed the Cajun Shepherd Pie he shares here from an old Louisiana recipe, playing around with the spices until he had them just the way he likes them—lively and zesty, like all of his cooking.

# CAJUN SHEPHERD PIE

**1 pound ground beef**
**¼ pound ground pork**
**1 egg**
**¼ cup bread crumbs**
**5½ tablespoons butter**
**½ cup finely chopped onion**
**½ cup finely chopped celery**
**¼ cup finely chopped green pepper**
**2 teaspoons minced garlic**
**½ tablespoon Worcestershire sauce**
**¼ teaspoon Tabasco sauce**

***Meat Seasoning Mix:***
**¾ teaspoon cayenne pepper**
**¾ teaspoon salt**
**¾ teaspoon black pepper**
**½ teaspoon white pepper**
**½ teaspoon ground cumin**
**½ teaspoon dried thyme leaves**

**1 pound white potatoes, scrubbed**
**¾ cup thinly sliced zucchini**
**¾ cup thinly sliced white onion**
**¾ cup thinly sliced mushrooms**
**1 cup shredded carrots**

*Vegetable Seasoning Mix:*
    **¼ teaspoon salt**
    **1/8 teaspoon white pepper**
    **1/8 teaspoon onion powder**
    **1/8 teaspoon garlic powder**
    **1/8 teaspoon cayenne pepper**

Preheat oven to 450 degrees. In a large bowl, combine the beef and pork. Mix in the egg and bread crumbs thoroughly. Set aside.

In a small saucepan, heat the butter, then add the chopped onion, celery, green pepper, garlic, Worcestershire sauce, Tabasco sauce, and Meat Seasoning Mix. Saute over high heat for about 5 minutes, stirring often, until vegetable are limp. Remove from heat, and cool. Add the sauteed vegetables to the meat, and mix well. Spread this mixture to cover the bottom of an ungreased 8-inch square baking pan. Bake at 450 degrees for about 20 minutes. Remove from the oven, and pour off the drippings into a skillet.

While the meat is cooking, boil the potatoes until they can be easily pierced with a fork. Drain well and mash until creamy and smooth.

In the skillet with the meat drippings, combine the sliced zucchini, sliced onions, mushrooms, carrots, and Vegetable Seasoning Mix. Saute 5 minutes until onions are limp and remove from heat. Mound the vegetables on top of the meat. Layer the mashed potatoes on top of the vegetables. Bake, uncovered, at 425 degrees for approximately 10 minutes, until hot. Serves 6-8.

# SHRIMP DIANE

**1½ sticks butter**
**¼ cup very finely chopped green onions**
**¾ teaspoon salt**
**½ teaspoon minced garlic**
**¼ teaspoon cayenne pepper**
**¼ teaspoon white pepper**
**¼ teaspoon black pepper**
**¼ teaspoon dried basil**
**¼ teaspoon dried thyme**
**1/8 teaspoon dried oregano**
**1½ pounds medium-sized shrimp, peeled and deveined**
**½ pound mushrooms, sliced**
**3 tablespoons finely chopped parsley**
**hot cooked rice**

In a large skillet, melt 1 stick of the butter over high heat. Add the green onions, salt, garlic, ground peppers, and herbs. Stir well. Add the shrimp, and saute about 1 minute. Add the mushrooms, and the remaining ½ stick of butter. When the butter is melted, add the parsley, and stir until the ingredients are thoroughly mixed. Serve immediately over hot rice. Serves 4-6.

## The Chalkboard
### 621 State Street, Santa Barbara
### 962-2773

The closing of the Grand Hotel in Los Olivos turned out to be fortunate for Santa Barbara, because it resulted in Chef Guy Bergounhoux purchasing his own restaurant and bringing his excellent food to town. I think he is one of the most talented chefs in Santa Barbara, but when I told him this, he just laughed and said: "You mean on this block."

Located right on State Street, the restaurant can be spotted by the chalkboard out in front. I like the decor, with its polished wooden tables, dark high-backed chairs, nice antiques, and a wall covered with menus from European restaurants. It evokes the atmosphere of a restaurant far from Santa Barbara, possibly because of the complete absence of the color pink. True to its name, entrees are written on chalkboards. The menu, consisting of about eight entrees, changes several times a week.

Chef Bergounhoux received his rigorous training in France. He developed the recipe for Gratin de Fruites-Rouge he shares here in Antibes at La Bonne Auberge. He says that April gives the biggest choice of red fruits for this light dessert.

After eating at the Chalkboard, I find myself remembering the meal vividly and longingly for days. Bergounhoux calls his food "Provencal cooking with American ingredients" and says that "the tastes of California affect the personality of the food." He certainly knows how to make California taste good.

# ESCALOPE DE VEAU A L'ANANAS (VEAL PINEAPPLE)

1 lemon
2 cups pineapple juice, preferably fresh
1 tablespoon grated ginger
1 teaspoon orange marmalade
3 teaspoons white vinegar
10 pine nuts
2 tablespoons butter or vegetable oil
4 veal cutlets, 4 ounces each, thinly pounded

Peel the lemon with a potato peeler and julienne it. In a saucepan, combine the pineapple juice with the lemon and ginger, and bring it to a boil. Cook until it has reduced by half. To this reduction, add the marmalade and vinegar, and bring to a boil again. Add the pine nuts and remove from heat.

In a non-stick frying pan large enough to hold all the veal, melt the butter or heat the oil and cook the veal over medium high heat for one minute on each side. Remove to a platter and top with the sauce. Serves 4.

# HALIBUT AUX AROMATES

**8 tablespoons Mariniere Vegetables (recipe follows)**
**3 tablespoons olive oil**
**4 halibut steaks, 6 ounces each**
**salt and pepper to taste**
**1 lemon or lime, peeled and diced**
**4 teaspoons chopped chives**
**few sprigs of cilantro (optional)**

Prepare the Mariniere Vegetables and keep warm.

In a large skillet, heat the olive oil over medium high heat and add the fish. Season with salt and pepper. Cook until just done, approximately 5-7 minutes per side. Divide onto 4 plates and place 2 tablespoons of Mariniere on each portion. Add a little diced lemon on top of each portion and sprinkle on 1 teaspoon of chives per portion. Garnish with cilantro, if desired. Serves 4.

## *Mariniere Vegetables*

**2 teaspoons olive oil**
**¼ red onion, medium sized, diced**
**1 stalk celery, diced**
**¼ red bell pepper, diced**
**¼ green bell pepper, diced**
**½ jalapeno, diced**
**1 tomato, diced**
**1 garlic clove, minced**
**¼ zucchini, diced**
**2 fresh basil leaves, slivered**
**½ teaspoon fresh thyme**
**5 black olives, pitted and diced**
**5 green olives, pitted and diced**
**1 tablespoon capers**
**1 pinch of saffron**

In a medium saucepan, heat the olive oil and add, in order, the onion, celery, peppers, tomato, garlic and zucchini, stirring and cooking briefly after each addition. Vegetables should still be crisp. Add the rest of the ingredients and heat briefly. Serves 4.

# GRILLED SWORDFISH WITH PAPAYA, MINT, AND GREEN CHILE SALSA

**Papaya, Mint, and Green Chile Salsa (recipe follows)**
**6 fresh swordfish steaks, 6 ounces each**

The day before serving, make the Salsa. Grill the swordfish steaks on a barbecue, grill, or in the broiler, until they are just cooked through, about 5 minutes per side. Top with Salsa and serve. Serves 6.

## Papaya, Mint, and Green Chile Salsa

**2 fresh papayas, roughly diced**
**1 small red onion, diced**
**½ cup green chilies, chopped**
**½ cup fresh mint, chopped**
**¼ cup fresh lemon or lime juice**
**¼ cup olive oil**

Combine the ingredients in a glass bowl and let stand overnight in the refrigerator. Makes about 3 cups.

# GRATIN DE FRUITS-ROUGES (GRATIN OF RED FRUIT)

**1 basket strawberries (or any red berries)**
**1 shot Triple sec**
**3 egg yolks**
**½ cup orange juice**
**2 ounces sugar**

Wash the berries. Quarter them if you are using strawberries, otherwise use them whole. Mix the berries with the triple sec in a large bowl.

In the top of a double boiler, place the egg yolks, orange juice, and sugar. Heat this mixture, whipping vigorously until it becomes foamy and a little thick. Remove from heat.

Put the berries into four ramekins (shallow individual souffle dishes) and cover with the egg mixture. Put under the broiler and cook until slightly golden, about 3-5 minutes. Serves 4.

## Charlotte
## 742 State Street, Santa Barbara
## 966-1221

By its name, Charlotte, the cafe, bakery, and restaurant on State Street, could easily be French, English or American. By its decor, with its brown paisley tablecloths, upholstered chairs, lace curtains, and cozy informality, it most resembles a genteel English tea shop.

In fact, the restaurant takes its name from the pastry Charlotte Russe, a layered confection of creams, fruit fillings and sponge cake. Owner Patrick Lesec is a master pastry chef, and when he and his wife, Carla Van Wingerden, opened the restaurant in 1981, it was primarily a bakery serving breakfast and lunch. Their specialty was Charlotte cakes.

Over time, the restaurant added dinners and grew to include a sophisticated menu, but the breads, croissants and pastries are still all baked on the premises. The bread served with lunch and dinner includes both French bread and a delicious, light, crusty wheat bread. Refrigerated cases in the rear display tempting rows of raspberry tarts, Napoleon Charlottes, pecan rum mousse, and chocolate raspberry cakes.

Charlotte serves a variety of dishes from meat to seafood to very original salads. Patrick Lesec, who grew up in France, describes his cooking as a mixture of Southern French and Italian, pointing out that a lot of the items on the menu are "original concoctions." For example, when baby zucchini flowers are in season, Patrick stuffs them with spinach, feta cheese, and herbs, and they are wonderful.

The recipes featured here include Fettuccine Colombo that combines ginger and red peppers to make a wonderful sauce for pasta with scallops. Veal Lasagna, which contains baby beets, is an unusual variation on a familiar theme. It is not baked, but rather assembled individually and served immediately.

Lesec is a familiar sight at the local Farmer's Market, which he has attended faithfully since it opened. He says he likes to go to check out new farms and crops. "It's a bounty to have a market like that. Fresh produce from good farmers is essential to anyone who wants to do good cooking."

# FILET MIGNON JARDINIERE

**6 Crepes (recipe follows)**
**12 baby carrots, peeled and sliced thinly**
**1 tablespoon butter**
**salt and pepper to taste**
**1 tablespoon olive oil**
**12 small Tokyo turnips, peeled and sliced thinly**
**1½ pounds filet mignon, cut crosswise into pieces the size of**
**    half dollars**
**1 bunch fresh basil, chopped**

Cook the crepes according to the recipe below and set aside.

In a small saucepan, add the butter, carrots, and enough water to barely cover. Season with salt and pepper. Cook on high heat, uncovered, until carrots are glazed (approximately 7 minutes; water will be evaporated). Do not over cook. Set aside and keep warm.

Meanwhile, heat the olive oil in a skillet, and saute the turnips for 2 minutes. Season with salt and pepper. Set aside and keep warm. Grill or broil the meat, until rare or medium rare. Season with salt and pepper.

Warm up the vegetables, if necessary, along with the crepe slivers and divide onto plates. Place the meat on top of the vegetables, and garnish with the chopped basil. Serves 4-6.

## Crepes
**1 cup all purpose flour**
**½ cup peanut oil**
**6 large eggs**
**1 cup milk**
**pinch of salt**

Mix all the ingredients in a blender. Let sit in the refrigerator for 3 hours. Pour a thin layer onto a buttered or oiled frying pan over medium heat. Flip when one side is cooked. Let the crepe cool, roll it up, and cut it into slivers. (This recipe will make more crepes than needed for Filet Mignon Jardiniere; you can use the rest, un-slivered, for dessert crepes.)

# *FETTUCCINE COLOMBO*

**1½ pounds fresh fettuccine**
**2 small red bell peppers or 1 large**
**2 teaspoons butter**
**1½-2 ounces ginger root, peeled and minced**
**½ cup fine white wine vinegar**
**2½ cups heavy cream**
**1 pound fresh scallops, Eastern or New Zealand**
**2 tablespoons olive oil (optional)**
**salt and pepper to taste**

Drop the fettuccine into boiling water for 1 minute. Drain and rinse with cold water to prevent sticking. Drain well and set aside.

Roast the bell peppers over an open flame, holding them with tongs, and turning them until the skin is consistently charred all around. Place each pepper in a paper bag and allow it to sit in the closed bag for 10 minutes to cool. When cool, remove from bag, peel, seed, and chop. Set aside.

In a small saucepan, melt the butter over medium high heat, and add the ginger, sauteing for a few minutes. Add the vinegar, and reduce the volume until it's the consistency of marmalade. Lower the heat, add the cream and the chopped bell pepper. Season with salt and pepper.

Place the reserved fettuccine into a large frying pan and pour the sauce in. Saute together over medium high heat, stirring frequently, until the cream gets thick but not oily.

While fettuccine and sauce are cooking, heat the oil in a skillet (or use a nonstick pan), and saute the scallops for 2 minutes over medium high heat, stirring frequently, until scallops are rare or medium rare. Serve the scallops on top of the fettuccine. Serves 4-6.

# VEAL LASAGNE

**1½ pounds ground veal, not too lean: 10% fat, ask butcher to grind it**
**1 cup ricotta cheese**
**2 ounces Parmesan cheese, grated**
**1 bunch baby beets (approx. 6), steamed, peeled and sliced unless very tiny**
**1 cup Veal Stock (recipe follows), or substitute chicken or beef broth**
**2 cups Tomato Sauce (recipe follows)**
**1 lasagna pasta sheet (13½" x 18"), preferably fresh**

Combine meat, ricotta, ½ of the Parmesan cheese, beets, veal stock, and tomato sauce in a large frying pan. Saute over high heat for 2-3 minutes, until veal is cooked through.

Cut the pasta into 12 squares, 4½" x 4½", and cook for one minute in salted, boiling water. Drain, rinse with cold water, and pat dry. Lay out the lasagna on a flat surface. Sprinkle the remaining Parmesan on top of 4 of the squares, and put under the broiler until light brown, 2-5 minutes. (These will be the top layers of the lasagna.)

Assemble the lasagna, while hot, on 4 separate plates. Place a layer of noodles, then a layer of meat. Repeat until all ingredients have been used, ending with the cheese-topped noodles. (There will be 2 layers of meat mixture inside 3 layers of pasta.) Serve immediately. Serves 4.

## Veal Stock

**2½ pounds Eastern veal bones**
**2 onions**
**2 carrots**
**2 tablespoons butter**
**½ cup white wine**
**1 small piece of cured ham or prosciutto**
**2½ tablespoons tomato paste**
**1½ quarts water**

**1 bouquet garni (1 scant teaspoon each of dried thyme, tarragon, bay leaf, rosemary, and 1 clove garlic, tied in cheese cloth)**

Preheat oven to 350 degrees. Place bones in an ovenproof pan and roast bones for 45 minutes. Meanwhile, in a stock pot, cook the onions and carrots slowly in butter for 20 minutes. Pour in white wine, and reduce liquid until dry, but not burnt. Put bones, ham, tomato paste, water, and herbs in the pot. Simmer for 3 hours, skimming very often. Strain the stock, and simmer for another 2½ hours. Makes approximately 1 quart.

## *Tomato Sauce*

**1 tablespoon olive oil**
**½ onion, chopped**
**1 shallot, chopped**
**8 ripe, medium tomatoes, peeled, seeded and chopped**
**1 tablespoon tomato paste**
**1 bouquet garni (1 scant teaspoon each thyme, rosemary, bay leaf, and savory, tied in a cheesecloth)**
**salt and pepper to taste**

In a medium saucepan, heat the oil and add the onions and shallots. Saute over medium heat for 15 minutes. Add the tomatoes, tomato paste, and spices, and simmer, covered, over low heat for 1½ hours. Stir occasionally, correcting seasonings if necessary. If sauce appears to thin, simmer a bit without lid on; if too thick, can add a little water. Makes 2 cups.

# *Chiang's*

**Chiang's
1046-K Coast Village Road, Montecito
969-0044**

The hands of the clock had crept past the hour of a timely dinner. We were both avoiding the kitchen. "Come on," I said to my constant companion. "We're going out." The CC sprang happily to his feet. "I have an inside tip on a great place I want to write about," I said. He sat back down. "Oh no, not me, I'm not going some place where they count the number of days since I shaved." (Upscale is not his style. If you can see the money, he'd rather not.) "It's Chinese," I reasoned, "how fancy could it get?"

I didn't tell him it was in Montecito, hoping he wouldn't notice. He did though, and grumbled all the way, only relaxing when he saw it was tucked away at the rear of the Von's shopping center.

Chiang's is a small, lovely, intimate restaurant, graced with the most comfortable chairs in town. The walls are decorated with beautiful Oriental instruments and prints, while paper lanterns hang down from the ceiling like moons over a Chinese garden. Morris Tang and his wife, Anna, took over the restaurant several years ago, after reading ads in Chinese newspapers and driving all over the country, looking for the perfect location for their gourmet Chinese cooking. A natural, gifted restaurateur, Morris, who sings Italian opera, has an easy affinity for his patrons—and the ability to listen to them. It was this that prompted him to remove all the MSG from his recipes, replacing it with herbs and spices. The entrees at Chiang's, more exotic than most, cover the whole range of Chinese regional cooking. The dishes are excellent in flavor and quality, and generously portioned too. Here Morris has shared his Duck with Garlic Sauce recipe, which is a house specialty and one of the "chef's vanities." The duck is marinated for two days and then steamed for hours, making it very moist and tender, as well as delicately flavored. The constant companion, who always orders spicy and sour soup, pronounced Chiang's as perfect. "It was just the right consistency," he said. "And I loved the mystery of the ingredients." Now the mystery is revealed.

## *SPICY AND SOUR SOUP*

**4 cups rich chicken stock, preferably homemade**
**3 tablespoons soy sauce**
**½ cup shredded bamboo shoots**
**¼ cup shredded wood ear mushrooms**
**¼ cup shredded white mushrooms**
**¼ pound cooked pork, shredded**
**¼ cup diced tofu**
**3 tablespoons vinegar**
**2 teaspoons chili oil or 1 teaspoon ground white pepper**
**2 tablespoons cornstarch**
**¼ cup water**
**1 egg**
**2 teaspoons sesame oil**
**1 green onion, chopped**

In a heavy pan, combine the chicken stock, soy sauce, bamboo shoots, mushrooms, and pork. Bring to a boil, and simmer for a few minutes. Add the tofu, vinegar, chili oil or pepper, and continue to simmer. Dissolve the cornstarch in the water, and, while stirring, add just enough to thicken the soup. (For a thicker soup, use more cornstarch.) Beat the egg in a small bowl and pour it slowly into the hot soup, while stirring quickly, to make "egg flowers." Add the sesame oil, and serve the soup in bowls. Sprinkle with chopped green onions. Serves 4.

# CHIANG'S DUCK WITH GARLIC SAUCE

**1 3½-4 pound duck**
**1 quart cooking rice wine ("Mirin," available at Chinese markets)**
**1 teaspoon salt**
**1 tablespoon sugar**
**1 bunch green onions, chopped**
**1 inch ginger root, peeled and smashed with flat of a knife**
**1 teaspoon pepper**
**Garlic Sauce (recipe follows)**

Defrost the duck, if frozen, but do not put it in water to do so. Cut off the tail bone. Combine the rice wine, salt, sugar, green onions, ginger root, and pepper in a glass dish large enough to hold the duck. Place the duck in the marinade. Cover and refrigerate for 48 hours, turning frequently.

Place the duck on a steamer rack in a wok and add water to bottom of rack. Cover and steam duck for 1½-2 hours, until cooked through. Let it cool.

Preheat the oven to 350 degrees. Skin and slice the duck, and place in a baking dish. Prepare the Garlic Sauce, and pour over the duck. Bake at 350 degrees until just heated through, about 10-15 minutes. Serves 4.

# Garlic Sauce

**2 tablespoons plus 1 teaspoon sugar**
**1½ teaspoons garlic powder**
**1 teaspoon ground ginger**
**2 tablespoons plus 1 teaspoon mushroom soy sauce**
  **(available at Chinese markets)**
**2 tablespoons plus 1 teaspoon soy sauce**
**2 tablespoons plus 1 teaspoon white vinegar**
**1½ teaspoons fish sauce**
**1½ teaspoons ketchup**
**1 teaspoon chili oil**
**1 teaspoon sesame oil**
**black pepper to taste**

Mix ingredients together in a saucepan, and bring to a boil. Simmer for a few minutes and remove from heat. Makes about ¾ cup.

# BEEF WITH DARK SAUCE

½ pound fresh broccoli, cut into small pieces
Dark Sauce (recipe follows)
1 onion, chopped
1 pound beef tenderloin, cut into thin strips
2 teaspoons cornstarch
¼ cup water

Bring a pot of water to a boil, and put the broccoli in for 30 seconds. Remove, drain, and cool under a little running cold water to stop the cooking. Prepare the Dark Sauce. Pour the sauce into a wok over high heat. Add the onion and stir-fry for 1-2 minutes. Add the beef and stir fry until cooked through, approximately 2-3 minutes. Add the broccoli, and heat briefly before serving.

In a small bowl, combine the cornstarch and water with a whisk. Add the cornstarch liquid to the wok gradually, stirring constantly until sauce is thickened. Serves 4.

Note: Any vegetable can be used instead of, or along with, the onion and broccoli, and you can use chicken or pork instead of beef.

## *Dark Sauce*

½ cup rich chicken broth
3 tablespoons mushroom soy sauce (available at Chinese markets)
3 tablespoons soy sauce
1 tablespoon sugar
1 teaspoon oyster sauce
1 teaspoon hoisin sauce
1 teaspoon vinegar
1 tablespoon rice wine ("Mirin," available at Chinese markets)
1 teaspoon sesame oil
1 teaspoon ground ginger
1 teaspoon garlic powder
¼ teaspoon ground pepper

Mix ingredients together in a saucepan and bring to a boil. Simmer for a few minutes and remove from heat. Makes about ¾ cup.

### Cold Spring Tavern
### 5995 Stagecoach Road, San Marcos Pass
### 967-0066

As you go up over San Marcos Pass, there are no signs to point the way to Cold Spring Tavern. Fourteen miles from Santa Barbara, you make a left turn on Stagecoach Road, just over the crest of the pass. Then keep going, farther than you think you ought, down a dark, winding, and sometimes spooky road. The sight of the tavern nestled in a bend of the road, is as welcome now as it must have been a hundred years ago to the bone-shaken stagecoach passengers coming over the pass.

In 1894 the place was known as the Cold Spring Relay Station where the "mud-wagons"—heavy duty stagecoaches used on the Pass—stopped to switch from four to six horses, while passengers had some refreshment. In the past hundred years, the distance to Cold Spring Tavern from Santa Barbara hasn't changed, only the forms of transportation used to get there. On a recent evening, the vehicles parked under the great elm and sycamore trees outside the old shingled tavern included both Mercedes and motorcycles. But no matter how they get there, once inside, everyone steps back in time.

The roof is almost low enough for head scraping, and the pine floors creak softly. In the three snug rooms of the tavern, huge stone fireplaces and kerosene lamps cast a warm glow on a museum of memorabilia. The walls are covered with old sepia photographs, Victorian prints, mounted deer, ram and bear heads, and framed homilies.

These items were collected and put there over the years by Audrey Ovington, whose mother, Adelaide Ovington, bought the tavern in 1941. They ran the place for many years. The current proprietor is Mark Larsen, who took over eight years ago. He and his chef, Ana Hanley, continue to attract visitors from all over the world and to keep their loyal clientele happy.

Beginning with the basics, the bread and water are delicious. For years the pure water, known as "Hobo Soda," was bottled and sold in the area. Their fresh baked Tavern bread, both the herbed garlic and the sweet whole wheat, could sweep all the prizes at the county fair.

The menu suits the Western roots of the tavern, and Mark and Ana take pride in the high quality of their steaks and prime rib, their Cold Spring chicken and their wild game dishes. The tavern is famous for its hearty Black Bean Chili and Cream of Chestnut Soup given here.

Legend has it there's a treasure in gold coins buried somewhere near the tavern by a couple of stagecoach bandits, hanged on the spot by a constable who forgot to ask questions first. But even without the lure of lost treasure, the old tavern exerts a pull on its visitors that is quite irresistible.

# BLACK BEAN CHILI

4 cups dried black beans
3 quarts water
1 tablespoon salt
1½ pounds lean, ground sirloin
2 medium yellow onions, diced
2 tablespoons finely chopped garlic
1 tablespoon chopped fresh rosemary
1 tablespoon chopped fresh sage
2 tablespoons chili powder
2 teaspoons cumin
5 serrano chilies, chopped
3 tablespoons arrowroot, thinned with ½ cup cold water
chopped onion and cilantro for garnish

In a large pot, cook the beans in the water, with the salt, until soft, about 2½-3 hours. Set aside.

In a large stock pot, saute the ground sirloin with the diced onions, garlic, spices, and chilies. Add the cooked, undrained beans. Bring to a boil, and add the arrowroot dissolved in water. Stir constantly, until the mixture boils again. Garnish with chopped onion and cilantro and serve. Makes 1 gallon.

# CREAM OF CHESTNUT SOUP

2½ pounds whole chestnuts
½ stick butter
2 large onions, finely diced
2 quarts rich chicken stock
1 tablespoon salt
½ cup honey
¾ teaspoon nutmeg
1 quart heavy cream
2 tablespoons arrowroot, dissolved in ¼ cup cold water
¼ cup toasted almonds for garnish

Preheat oven to 425 degrees. Cut slits in the shells of the chestnuts with a knife before roasting them in the oven for 15-20 minutes. Remove from oven, and allow to cool. Peel the chestnuts and chop coarsely.

In a small skillet, melt the butter, and add the onions and chopped chestnuts. Saute, stirring frequently, until onions are limp.

In a large saucepan, combine the chicken stock, salt, honey, and nutmeg, and bring to a boil. Meanwhile, process the chestnuts and onions in a food processor until pureed, adding a little chicken stock to thin if necessary. Add this mixture to the stock, then add the cream. Bring to a boil, stirring to make sure cream doesn't curdle. Add the dissolved arrowroot, stirring until it boils again. Serve sprinkled with toasted almonds. Serves 6.

# *RUM WALNUT CHOCOLATE CHIP PIE*

½ pound butter, melted
¾ cup granulated sugar
¾ cup brown sugar
6 eggs
1 cup flour
1 ounce rum
1 tablespoon vanilla
1¾ cups chopped walnuts
1¾ cups chocolate chips
2 10-inch, unbaked pie shells

Preheat oven to 350 degrees. In a food processor, process together the melted butter and sugars. Add the eggs, and process until they are absorbed. Add the flour to this mixture. Then add the rum, vanilla, walnuts, and chocolate chips and process briefly.

Pour the filling into the pie shells, and bake at 350 degrees for 35 minutes. Serves 12.

## Downey's
## 1305 State Street, Santa Barbara
## 966-5006

John Downey is a chef whose reputation in the food world sheds glory on the cuisine of Santa Barbara. His restaurant was recently awarded one of the very highest ratings given to Southern California restaurants by the prestigious *Gault Millau* guide, an honor shared by a very few.

Both *Gourmet* and *Santa Barbara* magazines credit Downey with introducing nouvelle cuisine to Santa Barbara in 1979 at the now-defunct Penelope's restaurant. Three years later he opened Downey's with the backing of another chef, Norbert Schulz. His long, rectangular restaurant, recently completely redecorated, is remarkable for the quality of the food and the enthusiasm it inspires in the staff. The menu, consisting of five or six appetizers and the same number of entrees, changes every day and is recited at the table by the waitperson, who describes each dish in precise and respectful detail.

Mussels with Chili Vinaigrette, featured here, is Downey's signature appetizer. Downey says that most of his ideas come to him in the shower, including the recipe for Chestnut Meringue Torte with Apricot Champagne Sauce. He wanted to do a light dessert to match a sweet wine at a winemaker's dinner. So after tasting the wine, he decided that apricots would go well with it. Because they were not available fresh at the time, he used dried. The chestnuts, however, were in season.

Recently Downey admitted that his cooking has changed considerably since those "crazy days of wild ideas and wild combinations that we all did. I've settled into better combinations of ingredients and contrasts of ingredients." What's wild today is how good his food tastes, and what's crazy now is how it makes you want to go back night after night to taste what's cooking.

# *MUSSELS WITH CHILI VINAIGRETTE*

**Chili Vinaigrette (recipe follows)**
**3 pounds medium sized, fresh mussels**
**1 cup white wine**
**3 bay leaves**
**3 shallots**
**1 teaspoon whole black peppercorns**
**½ bunch spinach leaves, washed and stemmed**

Make the Chili Vinaigrette. Discard any mussels that are open. A gentle tap may cause some to close, however, and these will be fine. Scrub the shells well and remove the beard, pulling it sharply to detach the part that is inside the shell.

Place the wine, bay leaves, shallots, and peppercorns in a kettle with a close fitting lid. Bring to a boil, reduce heat and simmer for 5 minutes. Add the mussels, and increase heat to high. Boil with the lid on until the mussels open. If, after checking, you find some of the mussels have not opened, return those to the kettle for a little longer, but discard any that continue to stay closed.

Carefully remove the mussels from shells. If sand is present, wash both the shells and mussels. Arrange the half-shells on a plate, like the spokes of a wheel. Place a small spinach leaf in each shell, then place a mussel on top of the leaf. Spoon Chili Vinaigrette generously over the mussels. Serves 6 as an appetizer.

# *Chili Vinaigrette*

½ tablespoon olive oil
½ jalapeno, finely chopped with a few of its seeds
½ small red bell pepper, chopped
½ cup cider vinegar
1 shallot, minced
1 teaspoon Dijon mustard
1 teaspoon Worcestershire sauce
freshly ground salt and black pepper to taste
1 cup extra virgin olive oil, mildly flavored
2 tablespoons chopped parsley
1 small bunch cilantro, chopped

In a small pan, heat the ½ tablespoon oil and gently saute the chopped peppers for a few minutes. Remove from heat, and reserve.

Combine the vinegar, shallot, mustard, Worcestershire sauce, salt and pepper in a small mixing bowl. Slowly whisk in the cup of olive oil. Add the parsley, cilantro, and reserved peppers. Allow to stand for at least one hour to marry the flavors. Stir again and correct seasoning if necessary. You may add extra jalapenos, but be careful! Makes about 1½ cups.

# BRAISED PORK LOIN
# WITH CIDER/SAGE SAUCE

**6-pound center cut pork loin (including bone)**
**4 tablespoons vegetable oil**
**1 medium onion, coarsely chopped**
**1 medium carrot, coarsely chopped**
**1 leek, coarsely chopped**
**2 stalks celery, coarsely chopped**
**6 bay leaves**
**2 teaspoons thyme**
**2 teaspoons sage**
**1 apple, sliced**
**1 cup hard cider**
**salt and pepper to taste**
**2 quarts good veal stock (or chicken stock)**

Have your butcher remove the bone from the pork loin and chop it into small pieces. Heat 2 tablespoons of the oil in an ovenproof pan large enough to hold the roast. Add the pork bones and saute until golden brown, 5-10 minutes. Pour off the excess grease, and add the chopped vegetables. Saute for another 10 minutes, stirring occasionally. Add the herbs, sliced apple, and ¾ cup of the cider. Add the veal stock, bring to a boil, then turn down heat and simmer gently for 1 hour with the cover on.

Meanwhile, trim the excess fat from the pork loin. Season well with salt and pepper. In a large skillet, heat the remaining 2 tablespoons oil over high heat and quickly saute the meat until brown on all sides.

Preheat the oven to 350 degrees. Place the meat in with the stock. It should be half covered with liquid. Place the pot in the oven, and cook for approximately 30 minutes. Turn the meat once after 15 minutes.

Remove the meat and keep in a warm place. Strain the sauce and correct the seasonings and consistency. Add the remaining ¼ cup of cider. Pour sauce onto 6 hot plates. Slice the pork thickly and arrange on top of the sauce. Accompany with warm Lentil Salad (recipe follows), or roast parsnips, or spinach braised with onions. Serves 6.

# WARM LENTIL SALAD

**1 quart good chicken stock**
**4 cloves garlic, minced fine**
**1 teaspoon rosemary, chopped fine**
**1 teaspoon thyme**
**3 bay leaves**
**black pepper to taste**
**½ cup best quality olive oil**
**3 teaspoons balsamic vinegar (or red wine vinegar)**
**½ teaspoon salt**
**1 tablespoon coarsely chopped fresh parsley**
**1 tablespoon chopped green onions**
**1 cup lentils, rinsed and picked over**

Place chicken stock, garlic, rosemary, thyme, bay leaves, and black pepper to taste in a 2-quart saucepan. Simmer gently for 15 minutes. Add the lentils and bring to a very light boil. Reduce the heat to very low, and cook slowly for 20-40 minutes until the lentils are just cooked. They should be "al dente," but not have that raw starchy taste.

While the lentils are cooking, whisk together the olive oil and vinegar in a medium bowl; add salt and pepper to taste. When lentils are cooked, drain well and add them to the dressing while still hot. Mix well. Add parsley and green onions, and serve. Serves 6 as a side dish.

# FRESH PAPAYA CHUTNEY

2½ pounds ripe papaya, peeled, seeded and cubed
2 ounces fresh ginger, grated
2 Anaheim chilies, seeded and julienned
1 sweet red pepper, seeded and julienned
½ jalapeno, chopped with seeds
2 small purple onions, julienned
½ bunch fresh mint leaves, chopped
1 bunch cilantro, chopped
¼ cup honey
½ cup lime juice
1 cup rice wine vinegar

Mix together the papaya, ginger, chilies, red pepper, jalapeno, onion, mint, and cilantro in a 2-quart bowl.

Combine the honey, lime juice, and vinegar in a small saucepan, and cook until reduced by half. Cool this mixture and add it to the fruit. Mix well. Let sit for at least an hour. Serves 16, allowing ½ cup per serving. Excellent with grilled duck, chicken, sausage, or pork chops.

Variation: fresh peaches or mango may be substituted for the papaya.

# CHESTNUT MERINGUE TORTE
# WITH APRICOT CHAMPAGNE SAUCE

Apricot Champagne Sauce (recipe follows)
8 ounces fresh chestnuts (buy extra to allow for rejects)
2½ cups heavy cream
4 ounces white chocolate, cut into chunks
12 meringue rounds, flat, about 4" in diameter
cocoa powder for dusting

Make the Apricot Champagne Sauce. Preheat oven to 450 degrees. Make a cross-cut in the flat side of each chestnut. Roast in the oven for about 15 minutes, until they open up. When cool, peel the chestnuts, then simmer them in a saucepan with 1½ cups of the cream for 30 minutes. Remove the chestnuts from the cream and set them aside to cool.

Add the white chocolate to the cream and allow to melt over low neat. When melted, remove from heat and blend in a food processor fitted with steel blades. Pour this white chocolate cream mixture into a clean container. Cover and refrigerate for at least several hours, preferably overnight.

When the white chocolate cream is thoroughly cold, add the remaining cup of heavy cream and carefully whip by hand until stiff. Do not overwhip.

Chop the cooked chestnuts and fold them into the whipped chocolate cream. Carefully spread some of the cream onto the uneven side of six meringues. Place the other meringues on top, with the smooth sides uppermost. Smooth the sides with a wide knife. Dust the top with cocoa powder and serve on a pool of Apricot Sauce. Serves 6.

## *Apricot Champagne Sauce* •

**3 ounces dried apricots**
**1 cup plus a little more champagne**

Soak the apricots overnight in one cup of the champagne. Puree in a food processor fitted with steel blades. Add the extra champagne at the last minute, adjusting to taste and consistency. Makes about 1½ cups.

## El Encanto
## 1900 Lausen Road, Santa Barbara
## 687-5000

I have always had a special feeling for El Encanto, the charming Riviera hotel with the romantic gardens. I love going to the restaurant, which reminds me of an old California home where elegance and comfort are a way of life. The gracious upholstered chairs, the well chosen shades of green, and the fine china and crystal all contribute to the evocative ambience. The great windows give a marvelous view, through the tops of stately eucalyptus trees, of the expanse of the city and sea below. On warm days, the step-layered terraces are filled with bright yellow tables for dining al fresco.

The food at El Encanto lives up to the setting. Lunches feature such dishes as Chicken Salad with Pears, Roquefort, and Tarragon Dressing; Pasta with Tomatoes, Chard, and Goat Cheese; or the Composed Salad of Spiny Lobster and Fresh Vegetables included here.

Dinner at El Encanto is an even more festive affair. The little golden lights on the wall sconces twinkle softly, while the lights of the city below twinkle back. The waiters sang "Happy Birthday" three times the last time we were there.

Chef Bryan Carr produces a new combination of elegant dishes for each day's menu, making each dish in effect a special. He has been in residence since October 1988, but the tradition of the daily printed menu at the hotel goes back for decades. While Carr's culinary training is French, the inspiration for his dishes comes from the best available local food products, from seafood and poultry to vegetables, fruits and cheeses.

The pastry chef is Heidi Mathieson, and her desserts are outstanding. Her Apricot Tart, which she shares here, is made unique by the use of cornmeal in the dough. She says you'll find it full of flavor and a fine finish to almost any meal.

# COMPOSED SALAD OF SPINY LOBSTER AND FRESH VEGETABLES

**¼ pound beets, peeled and thinly sliced**
**¼ pound broccoli, broken into small florets**
**¼ pound yellow squash, sliced**
**2 lobsters, 3 pounds each**
**¼ bunch radishes, sliced**
**½ bunch watercress, cleaned**
**1 bunch red lettuce, cleaned**
**¼ cup tarragon vinegar**
**1 cup olive oil**
**1 shallot, chopped fine**
**salt and pepper to taste**

Steam the beets, broccoli, and squash, until al dente. Chill in the refrigerator until needed.

Place the lobsters in a large pot of boiling water, and cook for 12 minutes. Cool lobsters in cold water for several minutes.

Remove the tail sections from the lobsters, peel and clean them. Slice the tails into 6 medallions each, for a total of 12 slices. (Use the rest of the lobster in another recipe.) Arrange the vegetables and lettuce on plates, with the lobster in the center. In a small bowl, whisk vinegar and oil together, and season with salt and pepper. Pour over salad. Serves 4.

Note: the proportions and variety of vegetables for this salad are variable. Choose brightly colored vegetables, some of which require cooking and others which can be eaten raw. Steam the vegetables which require it, chill and set them aside.

## *SEA BASS WITH FENNEL AND ARTICHOKES*

**6 medium artichokes**
**juice of 1 lemon**
**3 bulbs fennel**
**1 stick butter**
**2 cups white wine**
**6 sprigs fresh thyme**
**3 cups chicken stock**
**6 sea bass fillets, about 6 ounces each**
**1 cup heavy cream**
**salt and pepper to taste**
**1-2 fresh tomatoes, diced**

Trim the artichokes. Bring a large pot of salted water to a boil, and add the lemon juice. Cook the artichokes until tender. When the artichokes are done, chill in cold water. Remove them from water, pull off the leaves, and scrape the bottoms. Slice the bottoms thinly, and reserve.

Preheat the oven to 400 degrees. Clean and trim the fennel bulbs. Cut the bulbs in half, and place them in a heavy pan with the butter, wine, thyme, and chicken stock. Bring the liquid to a simmer on the stove, then place the pan in a 400 degree oven, and braise the fennel until it is tender, about 10-15 minutes.

When the fennel is done, place the sliced artichoke bottoms in the pan with the fennel, and put the bass fillets on top. Bake at 350 degrees for 10-15 minutes, or until the bass is done.

When the fish is ready, remove the fillets from the pan. Strain the liquid into a large saucepan. Arrange the fennel and artichokes on plates; put the bass fillets on top, and keep them in a warm place. Reduce the braising liquid in the pan down to 2 cups, then add the cream. Reduce to a proper consistency, and season with salt and pepper. Dress the fish with the sauce, and top with diced fresh tomatoes. Serves 6.

# CORNMEAL APRICOT TART

**Tart Dough (recipe follows)**
**1/3 cup ground almonds, lightly toasted**
**Poached Apricots (recipe follows)**
**powdered sugar for dusting**
**whipped cream**

Preheat the oven to 350 degrees. Take one rolled out round of tart dough, and peel off the plastic wrap from one side. Lay it across a tart pan, and gently press it into the form. Carefully remove the plastic wrap from the top of the dough, and trim the excess dough from the sides.

Sprinkle the ground almonds over the bottom to cover the tart. Place the apricots, overlapping each other, to fill the tart bottom. Wet the edges of the tart with water. Take the other half of the dough, and peel off the plastic wrap from one side. Lay it over the top of the tart, making sure to let the dough relax before pressing the edges together to seal. Carefully remove the plastic wrap and the extra dough from the sides.

Make a cross of little holes on the top with a fork to vent the crust. Bake at 350 degrees for 10 minutes; then turn down the oven to 300 degrees, and continue baking for 20 minutes more, until the top of the tart becomes a dark golden brown. Cool on a rack. Dust the top with powdered sugar, and serve with freshly whipped cream. Serves 6.

# Tart Dough

**1¼ cups flour**
**¾ cup cornmeal (sift before measuring)**
**1 stick butter, room temperature**
**1/3 cup sugar**
**3 tablespoons honey**
**2 teaspoons vanilla**
**2 egg yolks**

Combine the cornmeal and flour and set aside. In a large bowl, cream together the butter, sugar, honey, and vanilla. Add the yolks, one at a time, to the butter and sugar, beating with an electric mixer until the mixture is light and fluffy. Turn the mixer off. Pour in the dry ingredients. Then turn the mixer on at the slowest speed, combining the ingredients until they just come together. Split the dough into two equal parts. Roll out the dough between two pieces of plastic wrap, making sure that the circles of dough are a little larger than the tart pan. Refrigerate until firm. (At this point the dough can be refrigerated for several days, or frozen for up to a month.)

# Poached Apricots

**1 vanilla bean**
**3 cups water**
**1 cup sugar**
**¾ pound dried apricots**

Split the vanilla bean and scrape it into a saucepan with the water. Add the sugar and bring to a boil. Add the dried apricots, reduce the heat, and simmer for 25 minutes, until the apricots are tender, but not mushy. Remove from heat, and let sit until the apricots are cool enough to handle. (At this point the apricots can be stored, in the liquid, for up to 3 weeks, refrigerated.) Drain the apricots, and place them on a towel to remove excess liquid. Makes about 3 cups.

Note: you can substitute canned peaches, very well drained, for the poached apricots.

## Four Seasons Biltmore
## 1260 Channel Drive, Montecito
## 969-2261

In the sixties, I attended debutante parties at the Biltmore, and my husband and I had the rehearsal dinner for our wedding there, so naturally I feel that the Biltmore and I go way back. Still, every time I visit this historic hotel (it was built in 1927), I'm a little awed by its grandeur. And the new owners, the Four Seasons, have made it even more sumptuous.

The dining rooms at the hotel are elevated enough to give superb views of the ocean. This is where I love to go during big wave storms. My favorite dining room is the Patio, a vast solarium filled with a beautiful, diffused light coming through a stunning glass ceiling. You sit at glass topped tables in wonderful wicker arm-chairs, surrounded by full-sized trees and magnificent flower displays.

Chef Lluis Kaner grew up in Catalonia on the coast of Spain, and he trained in France and Switzerland before coming to this country. He is very comfortable with the meld of culinary influences that makes this one of Santa Barbara's most interesting restaurants. The menu blends California Cuisine (sweetbread salad with polenta croutons), with a little Italian (canneloni of chicken and veal), a little Chinese, (pot stickers), a little Southwestern (shrimp cocktail with cactus leaves and tomatillo sauce), and some traditional English/American dishes (prime rib with creamy horseradish and Yorkshire pudding).

The hotel serves hundreds of meals a day and recently remodelled its extensive kitchens on two floors. Chef Kaner boasts about his marvelous staff, and he gave me recipes from a couple of them to prove it. The roasted eggplant recipe and the Grilled New York Steak with Red Onion Marmalade were created by Mario Batali. Walter Kaiser provided the tuna (yes, it is not cooked) and pot stickers. The Paella a la Catalana comes from Lluis Kaner himself. It's a recipe from his native Costa Brava, which he calls "the Spanish national dish."

## *ROASTED EGGPLANT AND SWEET PEPPERS WITH FRESH MOZZARELLA AND SAGE*

2 whole eggplants, firm to the touch
olive oil for brushing on eggplant
garlic salt and black pepper to taste
4 tablespoons olive oil
1/3 bunch fresh rosemary
2 sweet red bell peppers
6 ounces fresh whole milk mozzarella in brine (available in Italian markets)
1 small bunch fresh sage, plus more for garnish
½ small bunch rosemary
1 tablespoon capers
1 bunch flat Italian parsley
4 ounces extra virgin olive oil
juice of ½ lemon
salt and pepper to taste

Preheat oven to 450 degrees. Cut the eggplants crosswise into slices that are 1 inch thick. (Each one should yield 5 or 6 slices.) Brush each slice with olive oil, and sprinkle with garlic salt and black pepper. Place the slices on a baking pan that has been brushed with olive oil. Bake in oven for 25 minutes. The eggplant should be soft to the touch, and the skin dark, but not black.

Combine the 4 tablespoons olive oil and 1/3 bunch rosemary in a small bowl, and let sit so the flavors infuse. Meanwhile, roast the bell peppers over an open flame, holding them with tongs, and turning them until the skin is consistently charred all around. Place each pepper in a paper bag and allow it to sit in the closed bag for 10 minutes to cool.

Remove the peppers, and peel the charred skin away under running water. Core, remove seeds, and cut into any shapes you wish. Pour the rosemary olive oil over them, and set aside.

To assemble, cut the eggplant slices in half, and arrange on the plate like the spokes of a wheel. Alternate the eggplant with peppers and slices of fresh mozzarella.

Make a sauce by pureeing the bunch of sage, the ½ bunch rosemary, capers, parsley, 4 ounces extra virgin olive oil, lemon, salt, and pepper in a blender, making a smooth paste. Thin, if necessary, with a touch of white wine. Spoon ½ teaspoon of the sauce over each piece of eggplant. Sprinkle fresh sage around the perimeters of the plate. Serves 4 as an appetizer.

## *NAPOLEON OF MARINATED TUNA WITH KOHLRABI, LEEKS, AND ORANGE SAUCE*

½ cup salt
½ cup sugar
½ cup black pepper
1 piece very fresh tuna, about 12 ounces
2 kohlrabi, blanched and sliced
4 ounces leeks, julienned
8 ounces orange juice
½ ounce orange zest, blanched
1 ounce rice vinegar
1 tablespoon cornstarch

Combine the salt, sugar, and pepper in a large glass dish. Add the tuna and marinate, covered, in the refrigerator for 24 hours, turning occasionally. Gently brush off the spices, and slice the tuna thinly.

In a small saucepan, bring the orange juice and orange zest to a boil and reduce to one half. Add the vinegar, heat through, and add cornstarch to thicken.

Put the orange sauce on the bottom of a plate. Put a layer of kohlrabi down, then a layer of leeks, and then a layer of tuna. Repeat. Serves 4-6 as an appetizer.

## POT STICKERS

**12 ounces ground pork**
**4 teaspoons ginger**
**4 ounces scallions, chopped**
**1 teaspoon Thai fish sauce**
**16 round won ton skins**
**1-2 tablespoons vegetable oil**
**4 ounces Pickled Red Cabbage (recipe follows)**
**4 teaspoons plum sauce**
**4 teaspoons Wasabi horseradish**
**4 sprigs cilantro**

Mix the pork, ginger, scallions, and fish sauce together. Fill the won ton skins with the pork mixture, moistening the edges to stick them together. Steam the pot stickers for 7 minutes.

Heat the oil in a skillet over medium high heat and saute the pot stickers until lightly brown.

On a bed of Pickled Red Cabbage, put 4 pot stickers on each plate. Garnish with plum sauce, wasabi and cilantro. Serves 4.

# Pickled Red Cabbage

2 cups rice vinegar
½ cup red wine
1 teaspoon anisette seeds
1 teaspoon hot pepper
salt to taste (just a little)
1 head cabbage, shredded fine

Mix the vinegar, wine, and seasonings together, and pour over the cabbage. Cover and refrigerate for several days before serving. Serves 6.

# *PAELLA A LA CATALANA*

2 cups vegetable oil
3 quail, cut in half
8 ounces chicken, cut in small pieces
8 ounces pork loin, diced
8 ounces fresh pork links, cut in half
2 medium onions, finely chopped
1½ tablespoons chopped garlic
2 tablespoons chopped parsley
2 cups diced tomatoes
16 ounces sliced squid
3 cups uncooked rice (not pre-treated)
5-6 cups chicken stock, approximately
1 pinch saffron
2 green peppers, diced
1 cup green peas
3 artichoke hearts (canned, fresh, or frozen, not marinated)
3 red pimientos, chopped
salt and cayenne pepper to taste
12 large, headless shrimp, shelled and deveined
18 clams
18 mussels
3 large lobster tails in the shell, cut into sections along the joints (live or use frozen)

Heat the oil in a pan and saute, in order, the quail, chicken, pork loin, and pork links until each is golden in color. Remove from heat and put in a colander to drain. When all the meat has been cooked, pour off all the oil except for about 3 tablespoons, and saute the onions until golden in color. Add the garlic and parsley, and mix thoroughly over the heat, without letting the garlic brown. Add the diced tomatoes, and slowly let the mixture cook down a little. Add the browned meats and the squid. Add a little of the chicken stock, and let it all simmer for 15 minutes. This is the base for the paella.

Note: The paella never waits for the guests; the guests wait for the paella. Therefore, 20-25 minutes before serving, preheat the oven to 375 degrees. Put the base into a paella pan, add the rice and stir everything together over high heat for a few minutes.

Add boiling chicken stock (equal in amount to double the amount of rice). Then add the saffron, green peppers, peas, artichoke hearts, pimientos, salt, and cayenne pepper. Rectify the seasoning. Arrange the shrimp, clams, mussels, and lobster tails on top of the paella. After cooking for 7 minutes on top of the stove, stirring often, place the pan in the oven at 375 degrees for 6 minutes, checking to see if the rice is cooked. Serves 6.

# GRILLED NEW YORK STEAK WITH RED ONION MARMALADE AND ROQUEFORT PEPPER CRUST

**Red Onion Marmalade (recipe follows)**
**Roquefort Pepper Crust (recipe follows)**
**4 New York steaks, 10 ounces each**
**salt and pepper to taste**

Make the Red Onion Marmalade and Roquefort Pepper Crust. Season the steaks with salt and pepper, and grill them a little rarer than you like, as they will be put in the oven to heat the crust.

Place the Red Onion Marmalade on the bottom of an ovenproof serving platter. Arrange the steaks on top. Spread a ½ inch Roquefort crust on top of the steaks. Bake for about 4-6 minutes in a 350 degree oven, until the crust gets hot. Serves 4.

# Red Onion Marmalade

**2 red onions, diced into ¼ inch pieces**
**2½ cups orange juice**
**2 tablespoons grated lemon zest**
**¼ cup dry vermouth**

Mix all the ingredients together in a small saucepan, and cook down over medium high heat until the onions are translucent. Serves 4 as a relish.

# Roquefort Pepper Crust

**6 tablespoons butter**
**½ sweet Walla Walla onion, diced**
**2 tablespoons freshly ground pepper**
**1 tablespoon fresh thyme or ½ teaspoon dried**
**1 cup toasted bread crumbs**
**¼ cup Roquefort or Stilton cheese, crumbled loosely**

Melt the butter over medium high heat in a small skillet, and saute the onions with the black pepper and thyme, until the onions are lightly browned. Add the bread crumbs, and cook over low heat for 25 minutes, stirring occasionally, until the bread crumbs turn the color of cookies. Allow to cool. Mix in the Roquefort, being careful not to break up the cheese too much.

## Franco & Rosa
## 225-E North Fairview Avenue, Goleta
## 967-3633

Franco & Rosa is set back in a small shopping center in Goleta near a movie theater. They've been so popular from the day they opened that they extended the restaurant by putting in a wall of greenhouse windows, giving it a very pleasant and cosmopolitan effect, even at night.

The restaurant is a relative of sorts of Pino's Italian Restaurant, also in Goleta. Rosa is one of the Pino family, and Franco used to cook for Pino's. And speaking of relatives, Franco & Rosa is full of them. When we were there one night, Franco and Rosa's son, Paolo, did a masterful job as maitre d', a nephew and sister-in-law waited tables, and Franco and Rosa did all the cooking while their youngest child was sound asleep in the back.

And they can cook. The smell alone of their dishes are mouth watering. The menu features seafood, chicken and veal in various Italian incarnations. There are 13 kinds of pasta, including home-made lasagna. Franco Miceli says that his Fettuccine Santa Barbara is his "creation to honor the beautiful Santa Barbara." The recipes here come from his own cookbook, which he sells in the restaurant.

It all smelled so good that we went overboard and ordered way too much. We asked for take home containers, which, happily, left us enough room for one of the great desserts in recent memory: Tartufo

Gelato, made with two flavors of homemade Italian ice cream, dark chocolate syrup in the middle, and whipped cream and cocoa powder on the outside.

We sat and talked, enjoying the end of a good meal. I watched the other diners giving heartfelt thanks as they left. We failed to notice when one of our group sneaked open a take home container and proceeded to polish it all off. Fortunately, he didn't eat mine.

# *VITELLO REALE (VEAL REAL)*

**1½ pounds veal scaloppine, pounded**
**½ cup flour**
**5 tablespoons butter**
**4 tablespoons garlic, chopped**
**4 tablespoons fresh green peas**
**8 marinated artichoke hearts, quartered**
**4 tablespoons olive oil**
**½ cup white wine**
**juice of 2 lemons**
**salt and pepper to taste**
**4 tablespoons parsley**

Flour the veal lightly. In a large skillet, heat 1 tablespoon of butter over medium high heat and saute the veal until done, about 2 minutes on each side. Keep warm.

In a separate pan, saute the garlic, green peas, and artichoke hearts in the olive oil and remaining 4 tablespoons butter. When the garlic is golden, add the wine and lemon juice. Place the veal on a warm plate, and pour the sauce over it. Serve immediately. Serves 4.

# FETTUCCINE SANTA BARBARA

1 pound fresh Fettuccine noodles
16 fresh basil leaves, chopped
4 tablespoons parsley
4 medium sized, ripe avocados, mashed
salt and pepper to taste
2 tablespoons olive oil
4 tablespoons butter
4 cloves garlic
4 stalks green onions
¼ cup grated Parmesan cheese, approximately

Cook the fettuccine al dente, and drain. In a large bowl, mix the chopped basil leaves, parsley, and mashed avocadoes. Add salt and pepper to taste, and stir well.

In a large skillet, heat the oil and butter, and saute the garlic and green onions over medium high heat. When the garlic is golden, add the avocado mixture and fettuccine. Toss gently while heating. Sprinkle with Parmesan cheese. Serves 4-6.

# AGNELLO ALLA CACCIATORE (HUNTER'S LAMB)

4 tablespoons olive oil
2 tablespoons butter
2 pounds lamb chops
8 garlic cloves, crushed
2 cups dry white wine
salt to taste
black and red pepper to taste
2 tablespoons capers
4 anchovy fillets
1 teaspoon oregano
1 teaspoon rosemary
2 bay leaves
1 pinch of sage
1 cup white vinegar

In a large pan, heat the oil and butter, and saute the lamb chops and garlic. When brown, add the wine, salt, peppers, capers, anchovies, and herbs. Cook for a few minutes on medium high, then cover, reduce heat, and simmer 15 minutes. Add the vinegar, and adjust seasonings. Cook slowly for another 10 minutes. If the meat is still not tender, cook for another 10 minutes. If it becomes too dry, add a little warm broth or water. This dish is good with polenta (corn meal) or egg noodles. Serves 4-6.

## *INSALATA TUTTO MARE (SEAFOOD SALAD)*

1 head Romaine lettuce, washed and torn into bite-sized pieces
2 fresh tomatoes, sliced
8 slices ripe avocado
12 whole black olives
3 tablespoons Italian Giardiniera (mixed vegetables in vinegar, available at Italian markets)
grated Parmesan cheese (optional)
¼ cup olive oil
4 ounces scallops, washed thoroughly
4 ounces shrimp, shelled and deveined
4 ounces clams, shelled
8 cloves garlic, chopped
4 green onions, chopped
4 tablespoons capers
12 fresh mushrooms, sliced
4 tablespoons white wine
juice of 2 lemons
4 tablespoons parsley, chopped
salt and pepper to taste

On a large salad plate, place the torn up lettuce leaves. Surround them with slices of tomato, avocado, olives, and Italian Giardiniera. Sprinkle with a little Parmesan cheese, if desired.

Heat the oil in a large skillet. Saute the seafood, garlic, onions, capers, and mushrooms until garlic and onions are golden and fish is cooked. Add the wine, lemon juice, parsley, salt, and pepper. Cook for a few more minutes, then pour on top of the salad. Serves 4 as an appetizer.

### Godzilla's
### 632 State Street, Santa Barbara
### 965-2980

I really liked the little smoothie bar on State Street, Smooth Choice, and was sad when it closed. So I watched the location with interest to see what would replace it. I've not been disappointed. Godzilla's showed up with something new in Santa Barbara, a combination sushi bar and robata (Japanese style barbecue).

The decor is streamlined and modern, but soft rather than slick. It has a long, elegant sushi bar and a combination of high perching tables as well as low ones, with lots of grey color and smooth, creamy wood.

The food is a novel change from the usual Japanese restaurant, offering a lot of surprises tucked into familiar forms. Take the miso soup for instance. I dubbed it a hearty miso; they call it miso chowder. It contains chunks of potatoes, carrots, clams and onions, and has a nice clam flavor on a base of miso soup.

The owners, Koji and Heather Numura, met one another at a Japanese class at the University. He is a sushi chef and she is the hostess, and they both sparkle with enthusiasm for their restaurant. Heather's mother-in-law makes the Godzilla Gyoza—homemade potstickers—which come with a wonderful sauce, called Ponzu Sauce. My son Teddy just loved them and is happy that the Numuras are sharing them here.

Besides the standard kinds of sushi, they have a number of original ones, like Roppongi, which has vegetables, crab and curry sauce, and the Godzilla, which is a deep-fried roll with spicy tuna, crab, asparagus and broccoli. The robata consists of skewered beef, chicken and fish, which are tasty and fun to share.

It's exciting when the cuisine of one culture gets inspired by another. The Godzilla Salad comes with fresh cucumber, broccoli, spinach, shrimp, Gobo crab (ground), tiny asparagus, and carrots. It has a dressing I would describe as Thousand Island meets the flavor of the Orient and the spice of the Southwest. I tried to get the recipe, but it's a secret. So then I tried the Say No More Salad, and I liked it even better.

My son Teddy, as usual, laid down the rules. "When we come back, we're ordering the salad, the soup, the gyozas, and one more thing. Then every time we come back, we'll order exactly that and one thing different." What an adventurer.

# GODZILLA'S GYOZA

**¾ pound ground pork**
**1 cup Chinese cabbage, finely chopped**
**1 tablespoon sake**
**1 cup green onions, finely chopped**
**1 clove garlic, finely chopped**
**1 tablespoon soy sauce**
**1 pinch salt**
**1 teaspoon sesame oil**
**1 package gyoza skins**
**Ponzu Sauce (recipe follows)**

Mix all the ingredients, except gyoza skins, in a large bowl. One at a time, moisten the outer edges of the gyoza skins with water and place approximately 1 tablespoon of the filling in the center. Fold in half, and pinch the edges together.

Steam the gyoza for 9 minutes or deep fry them for 2 minutes. Or you can cook in a frying pan, in a little sesame oil, for 5 to 8 minutes on low heat, until they turn brown. Serve with Ponzu Sauce. Makes 4 dozen.

# *Ponzu Sauce*

½ cup bottled ponzu (available at Japanese markets)
1 cup rice vinegar
¼ cup soy sauce
2" x 4" piece dashi kombu (available at Japanese markets)
¼ cup dried, flaked bonito or katsuo bushi (available at
  Japanese markets)

Mix all the ingredients together in a saucepan, and bring to a boil. Remove from heat, and cool to room temperature. Strain through cheese cloth or a cloth towel, and refrigerate. Makes 2 cups.

# *SAY NO MORE SALAD (SUNOMONO SALAD)*

½ pound shrimp, shelled and deveined
1/6 cup lemon juice
2 tablespoons sugar
1 cup rice vinegar
¼ pound octopus (sushi), pre-boiled
½ English cucumber (or 1 regular)
½ cup chopped broccoli
½ cup chopped asparagus
½ cup chopped spinach
¼ cup prepared gobo (yama gobo—available at Japanese
  markets)
¼ cup kaiware (available at Japanese markets)
Ponzu Sauce (see recipe above)
2 tablespoons dried, flaked bonito (available at Japanese
  markets)

Drop the shrimp into a pot of boiling water and boil for 1 minute. Remove and marinate in a mixture of the lemon juice, sugar, and rice vinegar for 1 hour.

Thinly slice the cucumber. If using a regular cucumber, slice in half first, and scrape out the seeds. Parboil the broccoli, asparagus, and spinach for 30 to 40 seconds. Cool. Arrange all the ingredients, including the gobo and kaiware, in bowls, and dress with Ponzu Sauce. Sprinkle on dried, flaked bonito. Serves 4.

# Ꜧibachi

## Hibachi
## 415 Milpas Street, Santa Barbara
## 962-2687

One of the pleasures of driving down Milpas Street over the past few years has been watching the greening of Hibachi. The vines that have now completely covered the pillars, and the wonderful bamboo plants have created an appealing little oasis of green around the restaurant.

We go as a family to Hibachi a lot. We seem to end up there at those times when one of us wants Italian, another feels like health food, one insists on Japanese and another refuses to even say what he wants. Then someone mentions Hibachi; harmony and anticipation are instantly restored.

Hibachi's owner, Mike Makino, is Japanese, but he lived in Honolulu for 12 years. His restaurant is patterned after the good, fast food restaurants common in Hawaii. You order at the window at Hibachi, and you can have your food to go, but I recommend eating right there; it's so casual and pleasant, both indoors and outside on the patio.

The menu consists of a combination of Japanese, Chinese, and Korean dishes. Even the pasta is essentially Asian, according to Mike, because Marco Polo brought the concept of noodles from China to Italy.

The variety of food at Hibachi is unexpectedly wonderful, ranging from delicious dim sum (Chinese dumplings) to Paella, and from Fettucine Clams to the Chicken Corn Soup featured here, which Mike says his mother used to make for him. The main entrees consist of chicken, beef or seafood, which can be ordered stir fried, teriyaki-style, as a kebab, or curry. The Stir-Fry Chicken is included here. Served with white or brown rice and a salad, it makes a meal that is both tasty and healthy.

Although we always agree about going to Hibachi, we can never agree on whether "Kane" and "Wahine" means "Men" and "Women" or vice versa. Maybe we have to argue about something, and we just can't argue about the food here.

## *STIR-FRY CHICKEN*

**12 ounces boneless, skinless chicken breasts**
**½ tablespoon ground ginger**
**1/3 teaspoon salt**
**1/3 teaspoon black pepper**
**1/3 teaspoon garlic powder**
**2 tablespoons vegetable oil**
**½ cup chopped carrots**
**¾ cup sliced zucchini**
**1 cup chopped onion**
**½ cup chopped celery**
**¾ cup sliced mushrooms**
**12 ounces bean sprouts**
**2 tablespoons oyster sauce**
**hot cooked rice**
**1 tablespoon teriyaki sauce**

Cut up the chicken breasts into small pieces. Combine the ginger, salt, pepper, and garlic powder in a small bowl and toss the chicken in it to coat thoroughly. Let sit at least 20 minutes.

Heat a wok and add the vegetable oil. When the oil is very hot, put the chicken in the wok. Stir fry the chicken until it becomes translucent. Add the carrots, zucchini, onion, celery, and mushrooms and stir fry. Add the bean sprouts and stir fry. Add the oyster sauce and stir fry briefly. Remove and serve over steamed rice. Sprinkle with teriyaki sauce. Serves 4.

# CHICKEN CORN SOUP

**6 ounces boneless, skinless chicken breasts**
**1 egg white**
**1 tablespoon sake**
**3 tablespoons cornstarch**
**5 cups chicken stock**
**1½ cups sweet creamed corn**
**1½ teaspoons salt**
**½ teaspoon white pepper**
**2 tablespoons water**
**1 egg**
**dash sesame oil**
**1 stalk green onion, chopped**

Cut up the chicken breasts into thin strips and mix in a medium bowl with the egg white, sake, and 1 tablespoon of the corn starch. Set aside.

Bring the chicken stock to a boil in a large saucepan, and add the corn, salt, pepper, and chicken. Mix the remaining 2 tablespoons of the cornstarch with the 2 tablespoons of water. Add this to the soup to thicken it. Beat the egg, and slowly add it to the soup in a thin stream while stirring gently. Add a dash of sesame oil. Remove from heat and add the green onion. Serves 6.

# La Super-Rica

### La Super-Rica
### 622 Milpas Street, Santa Barbara
### 963-4940

On a visit to Santa Barbara when I lived in Montana, my mother took me to lunch at La Super-Rica. It was a beautiful, sunny, winter day (twenty below in Montana). The trees were flowering (three months until spring in Montana). We ran into several people we knew (after three years, I hardly knew anyone in Montana). We picked up our food, and sat down in the patio. I took one bite of this magic Mexican cuisine, raised my eyes to the hills behind the restaurant, and decided to move back to Santa Barbara.

I have never regretted it. In fact, I go back as often as I can to La Super-Rica, just to celebrate that decision to move. This is also the restaurant where I take friends from out of town, when I want to show them something really special.

This small, unpretentious taqueria on Milpas Street doesn't even have a sign. It can usually be spotted by the line waiting patiently out on the sidewalk. You order at one window, and pick up the food at another—trying not to be too greedy with the fresh tomato salsa. Over the past years, the patio has become more and more enclosed. It now has glass sides and a canvas cover, which diffuses the light beautifully. It has plastic chairs, glass-topped picnic tables, and no decorations except for the plants, but the food is really the star here.

Isidoro Gonzalez, a former teacher with a master's degree in Spanish linguistics, had a dream of creating a really fine Mexican cuisine in Santa Barbara, and he made his dream come true. He is often the one taking orders at the window; his graciousness makes you feel like you've made his day just by showing up. But his real talent lies in the recipes he has developed for the taqueria.

All the food is served with freshly made, delicious, warm corn tortillas. You can order various combinations of fresh cooked meats, onions, green peppers, chilies, and wonderfully flavored melted cheese. Once Gonzalez perfects a series of recipes, he moves on to others. He developed the drinks for the taqueria, and is very pleased with the Hibiscus Cooler he shares here, having discovered that the drink is better when you let the flowers soak overnight. It's as simple to make as iced tea.

# *TACO DE HONGO (MUSHROOM TACO)*

**2½ tablespoons peanut oil
1 large white onion, roughly chopped
3 cloves garlic, chopped
1 large fresh tomato, peeled and chopped
1 pound mushrooms, well washed and thickly sliced
2 large sprigs of epazote, (an herb which grows wild, commonly found in Santa Barbara) or substitute fresh thyme
16 corn tortillas, warmed**

Heat the oil in a large skillet, and fry the onions, without browning, until soft. Add the garlic, and fry for a few more seconds, stirring constantly. Add the tomato, mushrooms, and epazote. Cover the pan, and cook over a low flame until the mushrooms are tender. They should be very juicy at this point. Serve with warm tortillas. Serves 8.

# ARROZ A LA MEXICANA

1/3 cup peanut oil
1½ cups uncooked long grain white rice
1/3 medium onion, finely chopped
2½ cups boiling water
1 large clove garlic, finely chopped
½ teaspoon dried basil

In a large pot with a tightly-fitting lid, heat the oil well. Add the rice and onions, and cook, stirring constantly, until both are lightly browned. Add boiling water, bring to a boil, turn down the heat and simmer, covered, for 20 minutes, or until the rice is done. Mix in the garlic and basil. Serves 6-8.

# SALSA VERDE

1 pound fresh tomatillos
4 fresh serrano chilies
6 sprigs fresh cilantro, roughly chopped
1 clove garlic
salt to taste

Remove the papery husks from the tomatillos. Put them in a medium saucepan, and add enough cold water to cover. Bring to a boil, and then drain.

Place the tomatillos in a blender, along with the chilies, cilantro, garlic, and salt. Blend until smooth. Let stand 1 hour before serving. Great on tacos, enchiladas, eggs, etc. Makes 2 cups.

# AGUA FRESCA DE FLOR DE JAMAICA (HIBISCUS COOLER)

¾ cup Jamaica flowers (available in Mexican markets)
4 cups cold water
1/3 cup granulated sugar

Mix the flowers, water and sugar together in a large bowl. Let them soak overnight. Strain the liquid through a colander into a pitcher. Taste, and add more sugar if needed. Serve well chilled. Makes 1 quart.

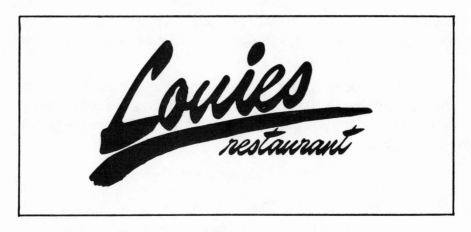

## Louie's
## 1404 De la Vina St., Santa Barbara
## 963-7003

Louie's at the Upham Hotel has the good fortune to be situated in one of Santa Barbara's most charming and historic buildings. The Upham Hotel, built in the 1870's, is a large, stately Victorian of great charm and grace. A visit to Louie's always gives me the pleasurable sensation of going "uptown" for a special treat.

Dining here is a special treat too. You can eat on the lovely wraparound veranda of the hotel, or in the cozy inside dining room. You can also have coffee after dinner around the fire of the hotel's sitting room.

The menu is fairly simple; it does not overwhelm with choices. But the food is imaginative, very fresh, and deliciously prepared. Tom Gilbertson opened the restaurant in 1984; his chef is Steve See. Gilbertson says that the aim of the restaurant is to use fresh local ingredients, such as those found in the Grilled Shrimp with Avocado and Fresh Tomato Salsa shown here. The cooking is based on French techniques, but the goal is to prepare it lighter. "The license is there in California Cuisine to mix things up differently," Gilbertson says. Thus you can find the successful coupling of pears and ginger with watercress and a slightly spicy, lime ginger dressing in the salad he offers here.

Louie's is also known for its light, savory pizza with delectable toppings, and the Pizza with Carmelized Onion and Gorgonzola Cheese is one of their most popular.

I like the latitude at Louie's. You can go for a light meal before or after an evening event, for a lovely lunch or a special occasion dinner. Or anytime you think you deserve something creative in the way of a good meal.

# WATERCRESS SALAD WITH RIPE PEARS, TOASTED ALMONDS, AND GINGER

**½ cup slivered almonds
6-8 bunches watercress
¼ cup rice wine vinegar
2 tablespoons white wine vinegar
juice of ½ lime
1 small finger ginger, grated
1/8 jalapeno, grated
¼ cup olive oil
2 tablespoons corn oil
salt and pepper to taste
2-3 ripe pears, any variety**

Toast the almonds in a 350 degree oven until they are slightly browned. Set aside.

Clean the watercress and remove the main stems. Mix the vinegars, lime juice, ginger, and jalapeno in a small bowl. Add the olive and corn oils slowly, whisking to emulsify. Season with salt and pepper. Add this dressing to the watercress and toss gently.

Divide the watercress onto 6 salad plates. Cut 9 wedges out of each pear and place 3 wedges on each plate around the watercress. Top with toasted slivered almonds. Serves 6.

# GRILLED SHRIMP WITH AVOCADO AND FRESH TOMATO SALSA

**1½ pounds medium-sized shrimp**
**salt and black pepper to taste**
**corn oil**
**Fresh Tomato Salsa (recipe follows)**
**2 avocados**

Peel and devein the shrimp. Season the shrimp with salt and black pepper. Coat the shrimp in corn oil (or any light oil). Thread the shrimp on skewers and cook 2-3 minutes on each side on a barbecue grill.

On small plates, place a layer of Salsa. Then put three wedges of avocado in the middle and 4-5 shrimp around the avocado. Serves 6-8 as an appetizer.

## *Fresh Tomato Salsa*

**7 Roma or Italian plum tomatoes, peeled, seeded and diced**
**1 bunch cilantro, coarsely chopped**
**1 clove garlic, chopped**
**½ jalapeno, grated**
**juice of 5 limes**
**salt and black pepper to taste**

Mix all the ingredients together and season to taste. Makes 1½ cups.

# PIZZA WITH CARMELIZED ONIONS AND GORGONZOLA CHEESE

**Pizza Dough (recipe follows, or use frozen pizza shells)**
**½ cup olive oil**
**4 large onions, diced**
**2 teaspoons sage**
**1 tablespoon thyme**
**salt and black pepper to taste**
**1 pound Gorgonzola cheese**
**½ pound mozzarella cheese**

If using homemade dough, make pizza dough.

In a large skillet, heat the olive oil over high heat until it has reached the smoking point. Add the onions, and cook until golden brown. Add the sage, thyme, salt, and pepper. Remove from heat and let cool.

Preheat oven to 400 degrees. Place the 8 pizzas on a lightly oiled sheet pan. Spread onions evenly on top of each pizza. Sprinkle with the Gorgonzola and top with mozzarella. Cook in the 400 degree oven for 7-9 minutes, or until the dough is a golden brown color. Serves 6-8.

## Pizza Dough

**5 cups all purpose flour**
**pinch of sugar**
**1½ ounces dry yeast**
**3 cups warm water**
**¼ cup milk**
**1 drop olive oil**
**2 teaspoons salt**

In a mixer, mix all the dry ingredients together, then add the liquids and combine. Let stand 5 minutes. Using the dough hook, mix at slow speed for about ten minutes, or until the dough is crawling up the dough hook. (The dough can also be kneaded by hand if necessary.)

Let the dough rest on a table for ½ hour. Divide into 8 equal portions. Roll into little balls and let rest another 20 minutes. Roll into 8 individual round pizzas.

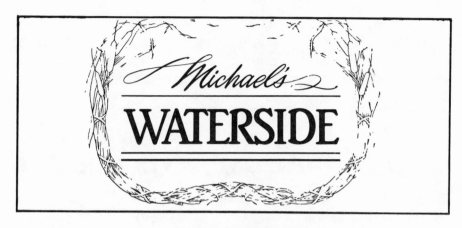

## Michael's Waterside
## 50 Los Patos Way, Montecito
## 969-0307

I like to think of Michael's Waterside as the Edwardian version of California cuisine—formal, elaborate and always in exquisite taste. I had a wonderful introduction to the restaurant last year when a good friend was writing a piece for the *Los Angeles Times* on Southern California brunches and took me there. Unfortunately for her, she had just acquired braces and could hardly chew a thing. Fortunately for me, she made me taste absolutely everything at the entire buffet, including every one of the desserts.

I think of that day fondly every time I drive by the Bird Refuge. Michael Hutchings' restaurant is truly "waterside," situated in an old house across from the lagoon, one of the most lyrical spots in Santa Barbara. A portion of the restaurant is in a large, stunning greenhouse attached to the house, which was moved from De la Vina Street in the sixties and dates back to the 1870's. The ambience is traditional and luxurious, with decorative wallpaper, upholstered chairs, mirrored columns, and elegant curtains. At night it's an oasis of candle-lit comfort, with the quiet hum of polite conversation mixing pleasantly with soft classical music.

Chef/proprietor Hutchings calls his food "modern French." Strongly influenced by his training in classic European cooking techniques, the complexity and variety of his dishes have given the restaurant one of the finest reputations in Southern California.

Michael's Waterside really is desert heaven, and the dessert menu is practically as long as the dinner menu. Hutchings said that he created his Sablé Heart's Desire, featured here, for a Valentine's Day menu several years ago, devising it for taste as well as color.

# *CULTURED ABALONE SANTA BARBARA*

**Beurre Blanc Sauce (recipe follows)**
**18 cultured abalone (2 inches in diameter)**
**salt and white pepper to taste**
**3 eggs**
**¼ cup milk**
**¼ cup flour**
**¼ cup cornmeal**
**4 tablespoons clarified butter**
**tomato rose and dill sprigs for garnish, optional**

Prepare the Beurre Blanc Sauce.

Prepare the abalone for cooking by running a small knife between the meat and the shell. Remove the intestines and cut off the head, located at the front area. Place the abalone foot between two moistened towels, and lightly pound to even them out and to tenderize the meat.

Season the abalone with salt and pepper. Combine the egg and milk in a small bowl and the flour and corn meal in another. Dip each abalone in the egg/milk mixture and dredge in the flour/cornmeal mixture. In a nonstick skillet, place the clarified butter over high heat. When it's very hot, saute the abalone quickly, about 10 seconds per side.

On a heated plate, put the Beurre Blanc Sauce, top with the abalone and garnish with a tomato rose and dill sprigs. Serves 6 as a appetizer. Note: Fresh shrimp may be substituted for the abalone.

# *Beurre Blanc Sauce*

3 shallots, peeled and chopped
1 cup dry white wine
½ cup whipping cream
¾ pound unsalted butter
1 teaspoon lemon juice
salt to taste
white pepper, freshly ground, to taste
1 teaspoon fresh dill, chopped
¼ cup corn kernels, blanched
2 teaspoons Roma tomatoes, peeled, seeded and julienned

Reduce the wine and shallots until almost dry in a heavy-bottomed, 1-quart saucepan. Add the cream and reduce by half over medium heat. Cut butter into small pieces and whisk, bit by bit into the reduction over medium heat. Do not boil. Adjust seasonings, add lemon juice, and strain. Add the dill, corn, and tomato. Keep warm while preparing the abalone.

# *WARM SQUAB SALAD*

5 tablespoons olive oil
1 cup peeled and diced sunchokes
1 cup sliced fresh shiitake mushrooms
2 cups boiled, peeled, and sliced yellow Finnish potatoes
6 tablespoons hazelnut oil
2 tablespoons sherry vinegar
½ teaspoon Dijon mustard
salt and fresh ground white pepper to taste
12 squab
lettuce leaves for garnish
chopped chives for garnish

Preheat oven to 425 degrees. Heat 2 tablespoons of olive oil in a skillet and cook the sunchokes on medium high heat until tender. Remove from pan. Add remaining 3 tablespoons olive oil and cook the mushrooms over high heat until done, about 5 minutes. In a large bowl, combine the sunchokes, mushrooms, and potatoes. Whisk together the hazelnut oil, vinegar, mustard, salt, and pepper, and toss with the potato mixture. Set aside and keep warm.

Roast the squabs in a baking dish for 10-15 minutes in a 425 degree oven. After removing from the oven, let rest 5 minutes. Bone and slice.

Dress lettuce on a large plate. Top with warm potato mixture. Arrange the squab on top, and garnish with chopped chives. Serves 12 for an appetizer or 6 for lunch.

# SABLÉ HEART'S DESIRE

**White Sablé Dough (recipe follows)**
**Dark Sablé Dough (recipe follows)**
**Chocolate Buttercream (recipe follows)**
**2 baskets raspberries, washed**
**1½ cups Sauce Melba (recipe follows)**
**mint leaves for garnish**

Preheat oven to 375 degrees. Roll out each color Sablé Dough to 1/8 inch thick. Cut out heart shapes with a heart cookie cutter (about 3½ inches long). You will need three hearts per person.

Place the hearts on a non-stick cookie sheet and, using a somewhat smaller heart cookie cutter, cut out the middle of each heart. Replace the white center with the dark and vice versa. Press gently into the dough to seal. Bake at 375 degrees for 10 minutes, or until the white Sablé is golden brown. Remove from oven and cool. Place one heart on a plate. Using a pastry bag fitted with a small star tip, pipe a border of Buttercream on one Sablé.

Combine the whole, fresh raspberries with the Melba Sauce, and place a dab of this mixture in the middle of the Sablé. Repeat this process with the second heart Sablé, and top with the third. Spoon a ring of the fresh raspberries and Melba Sauce mixture

around the plate and garnish with mint leaves and a few raspberries. Serves 12.

# White Sablé Dough

½ pound plus 3 tablespoons sweet butter, softened
1½ cups granulated sugar
2 egg yolks
1 tablespoon heavy cream
2 2/3 cups all purpose flour, sifted

# Dark Sablé Dough

½ pound plus 3 tablespoons sweet butter, softened
1½ cups granulated sugar
2 egg yolks
1 tablespoon heavy cream
2 cups all purpose flour, sifted with 1 scant cup unsweetened
  cocoa powder

The procedure for making the two doughs is identical. Do them
separately.

In a medium-sized bowl, cream the butter and sugar together.
Beat in the egg yolks and cream. Stir in the flour (in the case of
the dark sablé, stir in the cocoa and the flour which have been
sifted together), and mix well.

Using your hands, shape the dough into two rolls, each 2 inches
in diameter and 9 inches long. Wrap in waxed paper and refrigerate for 1 to 2 hours, until dough is firm but not hard. Excess
dough can be wrapped and frozen up to 2 months.

# Chocolate Buttercream

**3 ounces semi-sweet chocolate, chopped**
**5 egg yolks**
**1 cup sugar**
**¼ cup water**
**2½ sticks unsalted butter, room temperature, cut into ½ inch**
  **bits**
**2 tablespoons cocoa powder, sifted**
**1 ounce rum**

Melt the chocolate in a bowl over a saucepan of hot (not boiling) water.

Put the yolks in a blender and beat until light, fluffy, and lemon colored. Meanwhile, combine the sugar and water in a copper pot or heavy-bottomed, stainless steel saucepan. Cook over medium high heat, brushing down the sides with a pastry brush dipped in ice water, to the soft ball stage (240 degrees on a candy thermometer).

With the blender speed on low, slowly pour the cooked sugar syrup into the yolks. Beat at medium speed until lukewarm. This will take approximately 6-10 minutes.

Slowly add the butter, piece by piece. Add the melted chocolate, cocoa powder, and rum. Beat gently to blend. The buttercream is ready to use when cool, but not firm.

# Sauce Melba

**3 cups raspberries**
**¼ cup sugar**
**1 teaspoon lemon juice**

Rinse the berries and puree in a food processor or blender. Add the sugar and lemon juice. Push the mixture through a fine sieve. Cover and chill until ready to serve. This can be made ahead and frozen for use out of season. Makes about 1½ cups.

# MONTECITO CAFE

## The Montecito Cafe
## 1295 Coast Village Road, Montecito
## 969-3392

The Montecito Cafe is located in the Montecito Inn, one of Santa Barbara's historic hotels, built in 1928 by the legendary Charlie Chaplin. In true cafe style, the restaurant perches right on the sidewalk of Coast Village Road. Its many windows give it an unabashed view of the lively street known (to the horror of natives) as "Santa Barbara's Rodeo Drive."

Divided into two sections, one area of the restaurant has a wall of curved plate glass, a three-tiered fountain, and small marble tables. The main dining area, with its tall, arched windows, garden green chairs, snowy linen table cloths, and terra-cotta tiles, has the feel of a Tuscany restaurant.

Mark and Margaret Huston, both graduates of the California Culinary Academy, opened their restaurant in 1987 to almost instant success. Mark had previously been in charge of Brigitte's, where he developed a loyal following for his unique and memorable taste combinations. His menu features lots of daily specials, using the freshest food available at the moment.

Mark adapted the Goat Cheese Pancakes he shares here from a family recipe. They are the secret vice of many of his patrons. After trying this wonderful delicacy, lox and bagels will never be quite the same again.

# GOAT CHEESE PANCAKES

**6 eggs**
**1¼ cups flour**
**½ teaspoon sugar**
**3 tablespoons sour cream, plus extra for garnish**
**7 ounces goat cheese**
**1 tablespoon melted butter**
**thinly sliced smoked salmon**
**golden caviar for garnish, optional**

Beat the eggs gently in a mixing bowl, and add the flour and sugar. Add the 3 tablespoons sour cream and crumble the goat cheese into the mixture. Add the melted butter and stir gently. If the batter is too thick, add more sour cream. If the batter is too thin, add flour.

Spoon the batter onto a medium hot griddle, forming pancakes that are about three inches across. They should be golden brown when cooked. Garnish with slices of salmon, sour cream, and golden caviar, if desired. Makes about 24 3-inch pancakes.

# SPINACH SALAD WITH SCALLOPS, WALNUTS, AND CITRUS CREAM

**1 cup orange juice**
**juice of 1 lemons**
**1 cup fresh mayonnaise**
**salt and pepper to taste**
**2 bunches fresh spinach**
**1 tablespoon butter**
**1 cup fresh bay scallops**
**¼ cup chopped walnuts**

Bring orange and lemon juice to a boil and reduce until ¾ cup liquid remains. Remove from heat and whisk this juice into the mayonnaise. Season with salt and pepper.

Break up the spinach into small pieces in a salad bowl and toss with the orange dressing.

Get a saute pan very hot by putting it on high for a couple of minutes. Add a tablespoon of butter. (It will burn.) Then add the scallops, but do not stir. When they are brown, add the walnuts and stir to heat walnuts. Spoon over the salad. Serves 6.

# GRILLED SWORDFISH WITH LEMON BUTTER AND CORN RELISH

**Corn Relish (recipe follows)**
**6 fresh swordfish fillets**
**Lemon Butter (recipe follows)**

Make the Corn Relish. Barbecue the swordfish to your taste, about 5 minutes per side. Put a little Lemon Butter on each of 6 plates. Place a serving of fish over it and spoon 2 tablespoons Corn Relish on top for garnish. Serves 6.

## Corn Relish

**4 ears corn**
**1 red onion, diced**
**½ bunch chopped cilantro**
**1 jalapeno, seeded and chopped**
**4 limes**
**¼ cup olive oil**

Barbecue the corn. (A little charring is okay.) Cut off the kernels and put them in a bowl. Add the onion, cilantro, jalapeno pepper, lime juice, and olive oil. Stir well. Makes about 1½ cups.

## *Lemon Butter*

juice of 1 lemon
1 shallot, chopped
½ cup wine
½ cup cream
½ pound soft butter

Bring the lemon juice, chopped shallots, and wine to a boil over high heat. Reduce this liquid until only 1 tablespoon remains. Lower heat and add the cream. Cook over medium-high heat until it thickens. Remove from heat and add butter, whisking smooth. Set aside on the back of the stove where it is not on the burner but will keep warm.

## *GRILLED CHICKEN BREAST WITH ANAHEIM CHILIES, TOMATO, AND RED ONION*

1 red onion, thinly sliced
1 bunch cilantro, roughly chopped
2 cups whipping cream
3 Anaheim chilies, grilled to remove skin, seeded and sliced
   into small strips
6 Roma tomatoes, peeled, seeded, and chopped
salt and pepper to taste
8 boneless chicken breasts

Combine the onion, cilantro, cream, and chilies in a heavy saucepan. Bring to a boil over high heat, and reduce by one half. Add the tomatoes, and season with salt and pepper.

Barbecue the chicken breasts until the skin is crisp but the meat is still moist, about 3-5 minutes per side. Pour the sauce on individual plates and slice the breasts over the sauce. Serves 6.

## Mousse Odile
## 18 East Cota Street, Santa Barbara
## 962-5393

Mousse Odile has been a haven of French ambience and dining since 1980. Last year, it expanded a bit by opening up a charming little patio in the back of the restaurant. Nestled beneath a spreading loquat tree, with an old vine covered wall and lots of blooming plants, the patio is an oasis of tranquility. Under large green umbrellas, diners sit at small wrought iron tables with the restaurant's cheerful, red and blue plaid tablecloths.

Yvonne Mathieu and her sister, Odile, started out selling chocolate mousse from a small shop on Milpas Street. When they saw they were going to do well, they moved to their present location on Cota Street, a big pleasant space, divided into two sections. Their intentions were to stick with desserts. "But within a week we were open for lunch," says Yvonne, who has since bought out her sister's interest in the restaurant.

She also says that while the food is French, it is not unlike American food. "We French eat more vegetables, more salads, and more fruit," she says, "but the cooking is not that much different." The restaurant is, however, one of the few in town that serves rabbit, and her recipe for Rabbit in Dijon Mustard Sauce is a good example of the French cuisine bourgeois (home cooking) that is the specialty of the restaurant.

A bustling, popular, and casual place for breakfast and lunch, at night the restaurant is lit up with miniature lights and candles, and is transformed into a mode of elegance. It feels like France no matter when you go there. I love the food at Mousse Odile, and I especially love the patio, day or night. While eating delectable food in that peaceful enclosure, with the melancholy notes of a French song drifting through the window and the cheerful clatter of a busy kitchen in the background, anyone in Santa Barbara can go to France for an hour or two.

# *RABBIT IN DIJON MUSTARD SAUCE*

**1 rabbit, cut in 8 pieces**
**2 tablespoons olive oil**
**1 to 2 cups chicken stock**
**1½ cups burgundy**
**1 onion, chopped**
**1½ tablespoons Dijon mustard**
**3 bay leaves**
**salt and pepper to taste**
**2 tablespoons cornstarch, approximately**

In a large stewpot, heat the oil over high heat and brown the rabbit pieces on all sides. Remove the large pieces and cover the small pieces with stock. Add wine, onion, mustard, and seasonings. Bring to a boil, lower heat and simmer for 20 minutes. Add the large pieces of the rabbit. Continue cooking until the meat is very tender, about 1 hour. Remove the rabbit to a serving platter.

Take ½ cup of the stock and place in small bowl. Mix in cornstarch and stir to dissolve. Stirring constantly, gradually add this cornstarch liquid back to the simmering stewpot until the sauce thickens to desired consistency. Pour sauce over rabbit.
Serves 4-6.

# FILET MIGNON WITH
# PEPPER SAUCE AND COGNAC

**1 tablespoon butter**
**4 filet mignon, 4-6 ounces each**
**10-15 peppercorns, depending on individual taste**
**1 jigger brandy**
**1 cup heavy cream**
**salt and pepper to taste**

Melt the butter in a skillet and cook the steaks according to individual preference, about 7 minutes per side for rare. Remove the steaks from the pan, and place on individual plates.

Place the pan back on the flame, and add the peppercorns and brandy. Tip the pan so that the brandy bursts into flame. Add the cream, and heat for a few minutes. Season with salt and pepper, and serve over the steaks. Serves 4.

# CARROT SOUP

**10 carrots**
**¼ cup uncooked rice**
**1½ cups water or chicken stock**
**1½ cups heavy cream**
**salt and pepper to taste**
**dash of nutmeg**

Clean the carrots well, and cut the ends off. Cover the carrots and rice with water or stock in a medium saucepan, bring to a boil and then lower heat, simmering until the carrots are thoroughly cooked. Process in a blender until smooth. Return the liquid to the saucepan and add the cream, salt and pepper, and a dash of nutmeg. Cook gently over low heat until just heated through. Serves 4.

# Norbert's
## 920 De la Vina St., Santa Barbara
## 965-6012

Since coming to Santa Barbara in 1981, Norbert Schulz and his wife, Brigitte Guehr, have created a ripple of excellence throughout the Santa Barbara restaurant scene. In addition to their own two restaurants, Norbert's and Brigitte's, their former employees have gone on to own the Montecito Cafe and Oysters, and they also helped John Downey open his restaurant.

I had heard such wonderful things about Norbert's, I was almost too much in awe of the place to go there. I planned to go there when I sold my screenplay; I was waiting for my friends from New York to visit; I was saving it for my birthday. I finally realized this was silly. Do you wait to fall in love until you're eighty, just because you heard it was so great?

Located in an impeccable California bungalow, the restaurant, for all its elegance, has retained the feeling of a cozy, private home. Schulz writes out his menu daily, which allows him the greatest flexibility with what he calls his "seasonal creations," a fusion of the best available ingredients, his rigorous culinary training in Germany, and his wonderfully imaginative sense for food.

He says the recipe for Potato Pancakes with Sea Scallops, Avocado Mousse, and Tomato Salsa featured here is an example of this blend. The potato pancakes come from his European background, but the avocado mousse and salsa use typical Santa Barbara ingredients. However he blends them, his results are surprising, superb, and wonderfully satisfying.

Norbert's serves a seven course signature dinner that might begin with such dishes as breast of Smoked Muscovy Duck with Papaya, Frisee, and Hazelnuts, and end with his noted Chocolate Pecan Souffle with Papaya Ginger Sauce and Coconut Cream that I was pleased to get him to divulge. It's a memorable meal.

# POTATO PANCAKES WITH SEA SCALLOPS, AVOCADO MOUSSE, AND TOMATO SALSA

**Potato Pancakes (recipe follows)**
**Avocado Mousse (recipe follows)**
**Tomato Salsa (recipe follows)**
**3 tablespoons butter**
**18 medium sea scallops**
**salt and pepper to taste**

Make 18 pancakes according to recipe and keep warm until serving time. Make the Mousse and Salsa.

Melt the butter over medium high heat and saute the sea scallops until medium done, about 7-10 minutes. Season with salt and pepper.

Place 3 pancakes on each plate and add a little Avocado Mousse on each pancake. Put a scallop on each one, and top with Tomato Salsa. Serves 6 as an appetizer.

## *Potato Pancakes*

**2 large potatoes, shredded or grated just prior to cooking**
**salt and nutmeg to taste**
**¼ cup corn oil, approximately**

Combine potatoes, salt, and nutmeg. If the potato starch leaks out, mix it back in. Form about 18 small pancakes (about 1½ inches in diameter), and fry them on a griddle or in a pan in corn oil until they are crisp.

## *Avocado Mousse*

**2 ripe avocados**
**cayenne pepper, lemon juice, and salt to taste**

Peel and pit the avocados. Mix in the seasonings with a fork until smooth.

## *Tomato Salsa*

**3 large tomatoes, peeled, seeded, and diced**
**1 ounce cilantro, chopped**
**1 teaspoon chopped jalapeno**
**2 teaspoons chopped yellow chili**
**1 tablespoon red wine vinegar**
**salt and sugar to taste**

Mix all ingredients together. Makes about 1½ cups.

# ROASTED LAMB LOIN WITH FRESH HERBS

**1 lamb loin with bone in, about 4-5 pounds**
**fresh thyme and rosemary or oregano, chopped, to taste**
**Anaheim Chilies with Buffalo Mozzarella (recipe follows)**
**Lamb Sauce (recipe follows)**
**Blue and Golden Corn Cakes (recipe follows)**

Have the butcher bone the lamb. (You will need the bone for the Sauce.) Trim some of the fat off, but make sure to leave enough to protect it when you roast it. Sprinkle the loin with ½ of the fresh herbs, and keep it refrigerated until ready to cook.

Make the Anaheim Chilies to the point of placing in the oven.

Begin making Lamb Sauce. While sauce is cooking, preheat the oven to 400 degrees. Place the seasoned lamb loin in a hot, ovenproof pan on the stove top and brown on both sides. Remove pan to oven with oven mitts and roast at 400 degrees for about 10 to 15 minutes or until meat thermometer registers medium rare. Add Anaheim Chilies for last 5 minutes.

While lamb is cooking, make Corn Cakes. When lamb and chilies are done, remove from oven and keep warm. Use the roasting juices to flavor the Lamb Sauce.

Slice the lamb loin into 6 portions and place on plates. Sprinkle the lamb with more fresh chopped thyme and rosemary or oregano, and serve with Sauce, Blue and Golden Corn Cakes, and Anaheim Chilies with Buffalo Mozzarella. Serves 6.

## Anaheim Chilies with Buffalo Mozzarella

**6 Anaheim chilies**
**1½ cups fresh mozzarella, approximately**
**2 tablespoons chopped fresh chives**
**2 tablespoons chopped fresh basil**

Hold the chilies over an open gas flame and char on all sides. Cool in a paper bag and peel off skins. Seed the chilies, but keep them whole. Fill with fresh mozzarella, chives, and basil. Bake the chilies with the lamb loin, putting them in the oven about 5 minutes before the meat is done.

## *Lamb Sauce*

**lamb bone**
**2 tablespoons olive oil**
**1 carrot, chopped**
**1 onion, chopped**
**2 garlic cloves**
**2 ripe tomatoes, chopped**
**2 tablespoons tomato paste**
**salt and pepper to taste**
**1 cup red wine**
**1½ quarts vegetable stock (or water)**
**lamb juices**

Chop the bone into walnut-sized pieces. Roast pieces in hot oil in a pan on the stove until they are golden brown. Add the carrot, onion, garlic, tomatoes, and tomato paste, and continue cooking. Add salt and pepper. Add 1 cup of red wine, and reduce down to ¼ cup. Now add 1½ quarts of water or vegetable stock. Cook this down to ½ quart. Strain it through a cheese cloth, skim off the fat, and reduce it again to 1½ cups. Keep warm until ready to serve. Add lamb juices and stir.

## *Blue and Golden Corn Cakes*

**½ cup blue corn flour**
**½ cup all purpose flour**
**½ teaspoon baking powder**
**1 cup milk**
**½ cup fresh raw corn kernels**
**salt and a pinch of sugar to taste**
**butter for frying**

Blend the flours, baking powder, and milk to a pancake batter consistency. Add the corn kernels and the seasonings, and cook like pancakes on a buttered griddle. Keep warm until ready to serve. Serves 6.

# CHOCOLATE PECAN SOUFFLE WITH PAPAYA GINGER SAUCE AND COCONUT CREAM

Coconut Cream (recipe follows)
4 ounces butter
4 ounces semi-sweet chocolate
3 eggs, separated
1 cup chopped pecans
1/3 cup granulated sugar
Papaya Ginger Sauce (recipe follows)
powdered sugar

Make the Coconut Cream accoring to the recipe.

Preheat oven to 375 degrees. Melt the butter and chocolate in a double boiler. Fold in the egg yolks and chopped pecans. Remove from heat. With an electric mixer, beat the eggs whites with the sugar until stiff, and fold them into the chocolate mixture.

Butter and sugar 6 individual souffle dishes and fill ¾ full with the batter. Bake at 375 degrees for 20 to 25 minutes. While the souffle is baking, make the Papaya Ginger Sauce.

Take out of the oven, and with a small knife go around the dish to help remove the souffle. Divide the Papaya Ginger Sauce onto 6 plates. Place a souffle on each plate, and sprinkle a little powdered sugar on top. Place a scoop of Coconut Cream on the side. Serves 6.

## Coconut Cream

15 ounces cream of coconut (available in food stores)
1 cup milk
1½ cups heavy cream
½ cup toasted coconut flakes

Blend the cream of coconut with the milk, and add the cream and coconut flakes. Place in an ice cream maker and churn it for 30 minutes. Serves 6.

## *Papaya Ginger Sauce*

**2 small ripe papayas**
**½ ounce shredded ginger**
**zest and juice of ½ lime**

Puree the papaya in a blender, and add the ginger and lime. Makes about 1½ cups.

## Oysters
## 9 West Victoria Street, Santa Barbara
## 962-9888

Two of my best friends in Santa Barbara never eat at home after 11 am. I'm terribly jealous of them. You'd think we'd eat out together a lot, but they have their favorite spots, and sometimes I have trouble convincing them to try something new. They just can't see taking the risk of a disappointing meal when they can go to Oysters.

They love Oysters. With its simple menu of fresh fish, a little chicken, and steak or lamb, and a select number of appetizers, salads and desserts, Oysters suits their tastes and meets their standards.

Oysters was opened by Norbert and Brigitte Schulz, but they sold the restaurant to one of their chefs, Jerry Wilson and his sister, Loree, who is the manager. Young and very hardworking, these two are doing a fine job of maintaining the high standards of this restaurant.

On the edge of Victoria Court, Oysters is simply decorated, with green carpeting and snowy white tablecloths. It's one of those places that makes you feel well dressed even when you aren't. It must be the way the staff treats you. It has an open kitchen, a small wine bar, and a nice patio, with a good screen of trees partitioning it from the street. They also have a marvelous dessert cart you can keep your eye on as it moves around the room.

Yes, they serve fresh oysters—fried, grilled, and on the half shell. And their Oyster Stew is so perfect I just had to get the recipe. I think the hallmark of the restaurant is that they can cook fish to perfection, and their sauces are so imaginative and delicious. When I discovered tartar sauce in college, I was sure I had had a deprived childhood. Imagine my delight with Oysters' eggplant thyme relish, their tomato Brie cream, and their crab onion relish. The Strawberry Orange Relish with Spicy Orange Butter featured here is a truly elegant way to dress up a fish. The next time I make it I'm going to invite my friends over for dinner. But they'll probably want to go to Oysters instead.

~~~~

# CORN AND CRAB MEAT CHOWDER

**3 tablespoons olive oil**
**1 cup corn, fresh if possible**
**1 cup chopped celery**
**1 cup chopped leeks**
**1 cup chopped onion**
**1 tablespoon minced garlic**
**2 cups chopped potatoes**
**1 red pepper, roasted and chopped**
**salt to taste**
**cayenne pepper to taste**
**basil to taste**
**1 cup white wine**
**2 quarts fish stock**
**1 quart cream**
**2 cups fresh crab meat**

In a large saucepan, heat the olive oil over medium high heat, and saute the corn, celery, leeks, onion, and garlic until soft. Add the potatoes and the red pepper, and season with salt, cayenne, and basil to taste. Stir well. Add the white wine and enough fish stock to cover all the ingredients. Bring to a boil over high heat, then lower heat slightly and cook until the potatoes are soft (approximately 20 minutes). Add the cream, and heat gently to just below boiling point.

To serve, divide the crab meat, placing some in each bowl, and pour the chowder on top. Serves 8-10.

# OYSTER STEW

**4 tablespoons butter**
**8 shallots**
**12 or 16 Pacific oysters**
**1 cup chopped fresh spinach**
**fresh ground pepper to taste**
**2 cups cream**
**6 tablespoons Parmesan cheese**

Melt the butter in a medium saucepan over medium high heat. Cook the shallots in the butter until golden, and add the oysters and cook briefly. Lower heat, and add the spinach, pepper, and cream, cooking gently so cream won't curdle. When hot, pour into 4 bowls, sprinkle the Parmesan cheese on top, and put under a broiler or in a toaster oven to brown the cheese, about 3-5 minutes. Serves 4.

# STRAWBERRY ORANGE RELISH WITH SPICY ORANGE BUTTER

These sauces are excellent on any fish of choice, grilled, broiled or poached. To serve, put a little orange butter on a plate, place fish on top, and garnish with relish. Quantities given here are sufficient to serve with 6-8 pieces of fish.

## Strawberry Orange Relish

½ basket fresh strawberries, diced
2 oranges, sectioned, seeded and diced (prepare over a colander and save the juice separately)
juice of 1 lemon
1 tablespoon rice vinegar
1 tablespoon fresh cilantro, chopped
pinch of fresh ginger
pinch of crushed dried chilies
pinch of sugar

Combine all the ingredients in a bowl. Serves 6-8.

## Spicy Orange Butter

½ cup reserved orange juice from the Relish recipe
½ cup wine vinegar
pinch of chopped shallots
pinch of minced garlic
pinch of cayenne
pinch of paprika
pinch of curry
pinch of coriander
pinch of salt
pinch of Tabasco sauce
¼ cup cream
1/3-½ pound butter, cut into small bits

Combine the orange juice and vinegar in a saucepan over high heat, and reduce by half. Add all the seasonings and cream, and heat slowly until sauce is close to boiling. Reduce heat and whisk in the butter bit by bit, until the consistency of the sauce is thick and smooth. Serves 6-8.

## Pacific Grill
## 3765 Santa Claus Lane, Carpinteria
## 684-7670

You're whizzing along on the freeway when you see the sign. "Burgers" it says in great big letters perched above a homey little edifice. All of a sudden you feel a wave of nostalgia for the days when every hamburger place looked different and tasted different than all the others. When you could discover a place and then boast about it to your friends. When you could go in for a meal and come out with a sense of the owners and their aspirations.

Welcome to Pacific Grill.

The "Burgers" sign may grab the folks off the freeway, but the restaurant has also become a favorite for locals who have discovered that this pristine little place also offers good salads, interesting sandwiches, fresh fish, wine, and beer.

Sally and Alberto Rivera took over a former antique shop on Santa Claus Lane and transformed it into a simple, casual spot for a tasty meal. While virtually child-proof, the clean, blue and white decor sparkles with good taste. They've added some nice touches too, like fresh flowers on the checked tablecloths, wonderful Marcia Burtt landscapes on the walls, and a jukebox full of old favorites. Some people like to order their food and take it right to the beach to eat. Others sit out on the big patio overlooking the grassy, wooded yard leading to the beach.

The orange juice is fresh squeezed and the lemonade made from local lemons. The meat in the "three napkin burgers" is ground daily. They make their Tumacacori Chili with spices which Alberto imports from Tucson. They use it in their omelettes and their chili dogs, and people love it. Sally developed the Avocado Caviar and the Crab Avocado Salad recipes she shares for the annual Carpinteria Avocado Festival.

# AVOCADO CAVIAR

**1 avocado, cut in half with pit removed**
**¼ teaspoon garlic powder**
**¼ teaspoon white pepper**
**1/8 teaspoon salt**
**1 teaspoon lemon or lime juice**
**1 small jar golden caviar**
**tablewater biscuits**

Scoop out the avocado carefully, leaving the skin intact. Mash the avocado, adding to it all the ingredients except the caviar. Fill one half of the skin with the avocado mixture. Spread the caviar lightly on top. Serve with tablewater biscuits. Serves 4 as an appetizer, or 1 as a salad.

# ENSALADA DE AQUACATE FINCA DEL SITIO CUBA

**1 tablespoon lime juice, strained**
**2 tablespoons olive oil**
**1 pinch raw brown sugar**
**salt and pepper to taste**
**1 teaspoon rum**
**1 avocado**

Mix the lime juice, olive oil, sugar, salt, pepper, and rum together in a small bowl. Chill. Cut an avocado in half, and remove the pit. Fill the seed cavities with the dressing. Serves 2.

# TUMACACORI CHILI

3 tablespoons oil
1 onion, chopped
2 pounds beef, cut into small cubes
3 cups beef broth
1 16-ounce can tomatoes, chopped
1 teaspoon allspice
2 teaspoons cumin
2 teaspoons coriander
1 tablespoon oregano
1 teaspoon garlic powder
1 tablespoon tumacacori chili powder
1/3 can Santa Cruz brand pure chili paste
1 16-ounce can pinto beans
1 16-ounce can kidney beans

Heat the oil in a large saucepan, and saute the onion until soft. Add the beef, and cook over high heat for 3-4 minutes. Add the broth, tomatoes, and spices, and stir well. Add the beans, and bring to a boil. Lower heat, and simmer for 2-3 hours, stirring occasionally and adding a touch of water if chili gets too thick. Serves 6-8.

# CRAB AVOCADO SALAD

8-12 large lettuce leaves
2 tomatoes, sliced
2 avocados, sliced
7 teaspoons olive oil
2 teaspoons vinegar
1 teaspoon fresh lemon juice
3 tablespoons mayonnaise
1 teaspoon parsley
salt and pepper to taste
1 pound cooked crab meat or imitation crab, fresh or thawed
  if frozen
1/3 pound bay shrimp, cooked

Spread the lettuce leaves on a plate, and arrange tomato slices alternating with slices of avocado, around the edge. In a large bowl, combine the oil, vinegar, lemon juice, mayonnaise, parsley, salt, and pepper. Add the crab and shrimp, and mix lightly. Place seafood mixture in the center of each plate. Serves 6.

## The Palace Cafe
## 8 East Cota Street, Santa Barbara
## 966-3133

The Palace Cafe knows how to turn a good meal into a memorable one. It's a multi-ethnic, flamboyant, high intensity restaurant, enlivened by rousing music and a staff filled with incredible energy. They all seem to make every table their business. On weekend nights, patrons line up to get in, while being serenaded by a saxophone player on the sidewalk. Owner Steve Sponder says they finally opened up a second room in the restaurant because the regulars told them they couldn't wait anymore.

The new addition to the restaurant has my favorite mural in all of Santa Barbara. In it a glorious black man floats in rhapsody across the sky. The whole decor is a lot of fun here. Even the plates and serving platters come in whimsical fish shapes.

When The Palace expanded, they also built a bakery. Chef Scott Gibson started out as a baker, and the four kinds of fresh muffins they serve are whisked to the tables straight from the ovens. The light and wonderful Banana Walnut Muffins given here are one of his specialties. The bakery is also where they turn out their incredible desserts like the Louisiana Bread Pudding.

Sponder opened his restaurant in 1985, serving Cajun/Creole dishes at the height of the hunger for this regional food. He has since added Caribbean dishes to the menu, making it one of the most exotic and richly flavored mixtures of ethnic styles in town.

One day, I stepped out from the wrought iron balcony enclosed area of the main dining room in order to peer into the kitchen. The entire storage area consists of a modest stainless steel rack for spices and cans. All of the food comes in fresh, much of it flown in from the South and the Caribbean.

The enormous range was filled with cast iron skillets. Chef Gibson hefted up a huge skillet, and the entire mass inside flew up in the air, neatly rolled over, and redeposited itself in the pan. With a flick of the wrist he added something to another pan, and the entire contents erupted into flames. No wonder the restaurant is so exciting; they're just trying to keep up with the kitchen.

# *CHICKEN FRICASSEE*

¼ cup margarine or butter
1½ pounds boneless chicken breasts, diced
1 large onion, diced
15 large mushrooms, sliced
3 artichoke hearts, cut into thirds (fresh, canned or frozen, but not marinated)
2 teaspoons chopped garlic
1 teaspoon salt
½ teaspoon cayenne pepper
½ teaspoon white pepper
½ teaspoon black pepper
1½ cups heavy cream
3 tablespoon Creole mustard (or ½ Dijon and ½ grain mustard)
chopped parsley for garnish

In a large saucepan, combine the butter, chicken, onion, mushrooms, artichoke hearts, garlic, salt, and peppers. Saute on high heat, until all the chicken pieces have turned white, and the onions are transparent. Add the cream and mustard, and reduce heat. Simmer until it has reached the desired thickness. Garnish with parsley. Great with rice and vegetables. Serves 4-6.

# BANANA MUFFINS

4 cups flour
2 cups sugar
1 tablespoon plus 1 teaspoon baking soda
1 cup chopped walnuts
4 eggs
¾ pound margarine, melted
½ cup milk
2½ pounds ripe bananas, mashed

Preheat oven to 350 degrees. In one bowl, combine the flour, sugar, baking soda, and walnuts. In another bowl, combine the eggs, melted margarine, milk, and bananas. Then mix the dry ingredients with the moist ones. Spoon into muffin tins, which have been sprayed, or greased with butter, and dusted with flour. Bake at 350 degrees for 15-20 minutes or until a toothpick inserted in the center comes out clean. Makes 2 dozen.

# LOUISIANA BREAD PUDDING

½ pound sweet French bread, cubed
¼ cup melted margarine
1 cup raisins
16 eggs
1 quart milk
1 quart cream
1 tablespoon vanilla
¼ cup brandy
2 cups sugar
3 tablespoons cinnamon

Preheat oven to 325 degrees. Place the cubed French bread in a 14-inch x 14-inch baking dish, along with the melted margarine. Toss gently to coat the bread. Toast in a 325 degree oven until golden brown, about 10 minutes. Remove from oven. Spread the raisins evenly over the bread.

In a mixing bowl, combine the eggs, milk, cream, vanilla, brandy, and sugar. Mix well. Pour over the bread and raisins. Dunk the bread into the egg mixture until all the bread is saturated. Sprinkle cinnamon over the top.

Cover with foil, and bake at 325 degrees for approximately 1 hour, or until a knife inserted in the pudding comes out clean. Cut into pieces, and serve with whipped cream. Makes 16 pieces.

## Palm Terrace Cafe
## The Galleria, 2nd Level, La Cumbre & State Streets
## Santa Barbara, 682-2899

Tucked out of the way up on the second story of the Galleria shopping mall, the Palm Terrace Cafe is a festive mixture of art deco, California tropical, and designer cafe. The outcome is colorful, jazzy, and appealing. Maybe it's the art (they have paintings of cows, among others), but I always feel cheerful at the Palm Terrace Cafe.

Numerous potted palms adorn the different dining areas: a balcony terrace, a glass walled garden room, a small dining room with comfortable booths covered with fabulous, flashy fabric, and a long counter that seats diners on both sides.

Outside the entrance to the restaurant, tables have been set out under the remarkable skylight and geometric flags of the Galleria itself. Here, on the indoor terrace, one can sit and look down on the shops and shoppers below, becoming in fact the gallery of the Galleria.

The restaurant is open for breakfast, lunch, and dinner, even when the shops are closed. Owned by the Berkus family (architect Barry Berkus built the Galleria), the restaurant is now managed by Alfredo Arroyo, who changed the menu to include specialties of Mexico and Spain such as tapas, including the ones he has given here. Tapas are dishes that can be ordered as appetizers or entrees. In Spain, lots of little portions of various tapas are set out in the bars for patrons to nibble on while drinking.

The Palm Terrace Cafe serves some of the best nachos in town, very thin, fresh, and hot. The only problem is that it's not possible to stop eating them. They also have a terrific Caesar Salad and daily selections of fresh fish.

Alfredo Arroyo said that he and his chef came up with many of the new menu's dishes by experimenting together in the kitchen. Lamb Shanks with Tomatillo and Cilantro Sauce is one of the ones that gets the most "compliments to the chef."

## *TAPAS GAMBAS (SHRIMP IN A PASTRY SHELL)*

2½ tablespoons butter
½ cup chopped white onion
½ cup chopped red onion
12 medium shrimp
1 cup sliced mushrooms
4 tablespoons white wine
salt and white pepper to taste
½ teaspoon garlic powder or to taste
1 cup heavy cream
puff pastry dough, enough for two rounds, 5-6 inches across

Heat the butter in a saute pan. Add the onions and saute over medium high heat until limp. Add the shrimp, and cook for 2 minutes. Add the mushrooms, wine, and seasonings. Cook for 30 seconds, then add the cream. Cook until the mixture is somewhat reduced. Remove from heat, and keep warm.

Bake the pastry according to package directions. While still hot, slice it in half horizontally. Place the shrimp mixture on the bottom half of the pastry, and cover it with the other half.
Serves 2.

# TAPAS POLLO EN SALSA DE AJO (CHICKEN IN GARLIC SAUCE)

3½ tablespoons olive oil
1½ cups diced skinless chicken breast
¼ cup sliced red onion
¼ cup sliced white onion
¼ cup sliced red bell pepper
¼ cup sliced green bell pepper
½ cup chopped garlic
½ cup white wine
½ cup clam juice
½ cup tomato juice
salt and pepper to taste
1 teaspoon parsley, dried

Heat the olive oil in a skillet over medium high heat, and saute the chicken until just cooked through, about 3-4 minutes. Add the onions and bell peppers. Cook for 1 minute. Add garlic, wine, clam juice, and tomato juice, and cook to reduce sauce a little, about 3 minutes. Add salt, pepper, and parsley. Serves 2 as an appetizer.

# LAMB SHANKS WITH TOMATILLO AND CILANTRO SAUCE

5-6 lamb shanks
2 quarts beef stock
2 quarts water
¾ cup chopped white onions
3 cloves garlic
salt and pepper
Tomatillo and Cilantro Sauce (recipe follows)

Preheat oven to 400 degrees. Place the lamb shanks in a large ovenproof pan with the stock, water, onion, garlic, salt, and pepper. Cover with foil, and bake in the oven at 400 degrees for 3 hours. This will make them very tender.

Prepare the Sauce. When the lamb shanks are done, put them on a plate, and pour the Tomatillo Cilantro Sauce over them. Serves 5.

## *Tomatillo and Cilantro Sauce*

**9 tomatillos, with outer wrapper removed**
**3 cloves garlic**
**5 tablespoons clam juice**
**1¼ cups chopped fresh cilantro**
**salt and pepper to taste**

Cook the tomatillos and garlic, in just enough water to cover, for 10 minutes. Drain, reserving about 1/3 cup of the water. Puree the tomatillos and garlic with the reserved water in a food processor or blender. Return this to the pan, and reheat. Add clam juice, cilantro, salt, and pepper.

## *FILET A LA NORTENA (FILET MIGNON)*

**1 filet mignon, about 9 ounces, sliced into medallions**
**3½ teaspoons olive oil**
**2 jalapenos, seeded and sliced**
**¾ cup chopped tomatoes**
**¾ cup chopped, cooked bacon**
**½ cup red wine**
**½ cup tomato juice**
**½ cup clam juice**
**garlic salt and pepper to taste**
**cilantro for garnish**

Grill the medallions to your taste, about 5 minutes per side for rare.

In a separate pan, heat the olive oil, and saute the jalapenos until limp. Add the tomatoes, bacon, wine, tomato juice, and clam juice, and cook on medium high until sauce is reduced slightly. Add the medallions to the pan and heat. Season with garlic salt and pepper, and garnish with cilantro. Serves 2.

## Pane e Vino
## 1482 East Valley Road, Montecito
## 969-9274

The first time I tried to go to Pane e Vino it was closed—a Sunday. The second time, it was too crowded to accommodate us. So the third time, I called ahead and showed up early in the evening, before the restaurant filled up.

This little restaurant has been a great success almost from the day it opened. The place is always packed with a variety of people, from the crustiest of upper crusts to toddler tourists, all of them looking very happy with their Italian food.

I love the decor. If I were redoing my kitchen I'd send the designer over to Pane e Vino to see the warm gleaming wood, the green and black marble, and the white and green floor. I wouldn't mind the cases filled with cheeses, salamis, and antipasto either, or the shelves lined with bottles of straw-wrapped Chianti and imported Italian foods. The Italians can make a can of tomatoes look like a work of art.

And these Italians, Pietro Bernardi and chef Claudio Marchesan, make food that really delights. Marchesan came here from Prego, which he started in Los Angeles. It was their loss. His food is authentic, non-pretentious, and delicious.

My son hates tomatoes, hates spaghetti, won't eat garlic, and disdains basil. But when I passed him my plate of Capellini al

Pomodoro Naturale, to "just try a bite for me," he ate practically the whole thing. "For some reason I like this," he commented.

I love their Pollo all'Aglio e Rosmarino (Chicken with Garlic and Rosemary) and the Tiramisu, both of which are described here. Claudio says the Tiramisu is their own version of a classic Italian dessert. "Some like it more creamy, some like it less," he says. "Mine is in the middle. That's why it's so successful."

# CAPELLINI AL POMODORO NATURALE (ANGEL HAIR PASTA WITH FRESH TOMATO AND BASIL)

**4 medium, ripe tomatoes**
**3 ounces garlic**
**1 bunch fresh basil**
**½-¾ cup extra virgin olive oil**
**salt and pepper**
**12 ounces angel hair pasta—preferably the dry, store bought**
    **variety**
**grated Parmesan cheese (optional)**

Peel the tomatoes by dunking them in boiling water briefly. Dice them. Peel and slice the garlic in big slivers. Wash the basil, and break it into big pieces. Do not chop it.

In a saute pan, heat the olive oil, and add the tomatoes, garlic, basil, and salt and pepper to taste. Saute briefly over medium heat so that the ingredients blend together. Remove from heat before the tomatoes have a chance to get mushy. They should be only slightly more than warm.

Cook the capellini in plenty of boiling water until it is al dente. Do not over cook. Toss the pasta with the sauce and serve with Parmesan cheese, if desired. Serves 6.

# *PANZANELLA (TUSCAN SUMMER SALAD)*

1 loaf round Italian bread, a day or two old
1 cup beef stock
4-6 medium tomatoes, cut into wedges
2 cucumbers, peeled and sliced
1 bunch scallions, julienned
1 bunch fresh basil, chopped
3 ounces extra virgin olive oil
1½ ounce good wine vinegar
salt and pepper to taste

Remove the crust from the bread and dice it so the chunks are a little bigger than the size of playing dice. Put in a large bowl. Take a brush, dip it in the beef stock, then brush it on the bread to moisten it. Repeat until bread is moist but not soft. Add the tomatoes, cucumbers, scallions, and basil to the bread. Add the oil, vinegar, salt, and pepper, and toss. The salad should be well-coated, but not soaked. Cover with plastic wrap, and refrigerate for at least an hour before serving. Just before serving, scoop the juice up from the bottom of the bowl, and pour over the salad. Serves 6.

# *POLLO ALL'AGLIO E ROSMARINO (CHICKEN WITH GARLIC AND ROSEMARY)*

½ pound garlic
2 bunches Italian parsley, chopped
½ bunch fresh rosemary leaves, chopped
salt and pepper to taste
6 chicken breasts, boneless but with the skin on
1 cup butter
juice of one lemon
2 tablespoons white wine

Cut the garlic lengthwise into paper thin slices. Combine the garlic, parsley, rosemary, salt, and pepper. Stuff 1/2 of this mixture underneath the skins of the chicken breasts. Save the other half for the sauce. Grill the chicken over mesquite or charcoal, until the skin is crispy and well-marked, but the meat is still moist, about 5 minutes per side.

In a saute pan, melt the butter and add the other half of the herbs. When the mixture is sizzling, add the wine and lemon juice, and cook for a couple minutes. Put the chicken on plates, pour the sauce over, and serve. Serves 6.

## TIRAMISU

**1 pound mascarpone cheese (or unsalted cream cheese)**
**3 cups whipping cream**
**1 cup sugar**
**6 egg yolks**
**1 teaspoon vanilla**
**2 packages of Italian lady fingers (cookies, available at Italian markets)**
**2 cups brewed espresso**
**½ cup cocoa powder**
**mocca beans (a chocolate confection in the shape of coffee beans, available at specialty stores), optional**

Put the cheese and the whipping cream in a mixing bowl. Add the sugar, egg yolks, and vanilla, and whip with an electric mixer until the mixture has the consistency of whipped cream.

Soak the lady fingers briefly on both sides in the espresso. (There should be a dry portion in the middle of each cookie). Line a deep dish with a layer of cookies. Spread one inch of the cream on top (the same thickness as the cookies). Repeat until all cookies and cream are gone, ending with cream. With a little tea strainer or very fine sieve, sprinkle a generous amount of cocoa powder over the top. Make little designs with dollops of cream around the edges, and garnish with mocca beans, if desired. Serves 10.

## Papagallo's
## 731 De la Guerra Plaza, Santa Barbara
## 963-8374

Papagallo's takes its name from a large, colorful tropical bird that lives in the Amazon. Like its namesake, Papagallo's is a rare bird among Santa Barbara restaurants, exotic, unique, and truly foreign. Its Peruvian dishes have given Santa Barbara a different taste of South American regional cooking.

Jorge Ricci, a native Peruvian whose grandfather came from Italy, opened Papagallo's in Isla Vista in 1983. He decided to move downtown after taking pity on most of his patrons, who were driving out from Santa Barbara and Montecito. The restaurant is now on De la Guerra Plaza. Jorge's wife, Laura, works at the restaurant several nights a week and both his father and daughter are common fixtures, lending a nice sense of family.

A spacious courtyard with wrought iron tables and chairs and a trickling fountain give Papagallo's an old world ambience. Inside, the restaurant is small, cozy, and exotic. A room of many textures, it has a terra cotta floor, hand painted wooden chairs, one wall of brick, and another painted with a lovely blend of pastels. On a third wall, painted blue, a large pink "Papagallo's," written in neon, casts a warm glow on the room.

Old stringed instruments hanging on the wall reflect the restaurant's interest in music. Tapes of South American music play constantly. On weekends, weather permitting, there is live music on the patio.

The food is just delicious, fragrant with herbs and racing with spices. The pasta dishes, such as Fettucine Papagallo's, and the wonderful Milanesa, a thin breaded steak with lemon, owe their origins to Jorge's Italian heritage. The ones described here—Causa de Atun, Escabeche, and Lomito Saltado—are typical Peruvian favorites. Lomito Saltado in particular exemplifies the way Papagallo's cuisine blends spices and flavors so exquisitely.

At a recent wonderful dinner at the restaurant, I watched a family at another table. The little girl was happily eating tidbits as fast as her parents could give them to her. They had shoved their own dinners away from her, to keep her from plunging her eager hands into their plates. I knew just how she felt.

# ESCABECHE (FISH MARINATED IN ONIONS)

**6 fillets white fish, about 6 ounces each**
**salt and pepper to taste**
**2-3 tablespoons flour**
**3-4 tablespoons vegetable oil**
**lettuce or greens for garnish**
**2 large red onions, sliced thick**
**1 teaspoon ground fresh red chili powder**
**2 fresh green chilies, sliced into strips**
**1 teaspoon ground fresh garlic**
**½ cup red vinegar**
**4 hard boiled eggs, halved**
**4-5 black olives**
**parsley or cilantro for garnish**

Season the fish with salt and pepper, and dip into the flour. In a large skillet, heat 3 tablespoons of oil, and fry the fish over medium high heat until golden brown. Place fish on a serving dish that has been lined with lettuce.

In the same pan, saute the onion, chili powder, chilies, garlic, salt, and pepper in enough oil to coat the ingredients well (add more if needed). Saute over medium high heat until the onions are bright pink and a bit soft. Add the vinegar, and cover for a minute. Remove sauce from heat, and pour over the fish. Serve chilled or at room temperature. Garnish with eggs, olives, and parsley or cilantro. Serves 6.

# CAUSA DE ATUN (POTATOES AND TUNA)

**1 red onion, chopped**
**juice of 5 limes or lemons**
**salt and pepper to taste**
**1 teaspoon fresh ground chili powder**
**3 pounds yellow potatoes**
**1 tablespoon vegetable oil, approximately**
**2 6½-ounce can tuna**
**½ cup mayonnaise**
**1 small red onion, minced**
**1 teaspoon ground garlic**
**juice from 1 lime**
**10 black olives**
**1 red bell pepper, sliced**
**3 hard boiled eggs, halved**
**3 fresh chilies, sliced**

Marinate the onion in the juice of 4 limes or lemons combined with salt, pepper, and chili powder. Set aside. Boil the potatoes with the skins on. When tender, peel and mash. Add the

lime/onion mixture and mix, adding enough oil to make a smooth mixture. Set aside.

Drain the tuna, and combine with the mayonnaise, minced onion, ground garlic, and juice of 1 lime. Season with salt and pepper. Set aside.

Divide the potato mixture into two parts. Grease or oil the bottom of an 8-cup mold. Put half the potatoes into the mold.

Cover with the tuna filling. Finish with the remaining potatoes. Smooth out the top, and refrigerate for 1½ hours.

Flip the mold onto a serving plate, and garnish with olives, red pepper, hard boiled eggs and sliced chilies. Serves 6.

# *LOMITO SALTADO (BEEF WITH POTATOES, CHILI AND ONION)*

**2 large potatoes**
**2 tablespoons oil**
**1 pound beef tenderloin, cut into thin strips**
**1 large red onion, sliced thick**
**salt and pepper to taste**
**1 green chili, chopped or ground**
**2 tablespoons vinegar**
**1 teaspoon ground fresh garlic**
**cumin to taste**
**1 large tomato, cut into wedges**
**soy sauce to taste**
**cilantro for garnish**

Cut up the potatoes and french fry them, following any standard recipe. Set aside.

In a large skillet, heat the oil and cook the meat for 2-3 minutes. Add the onion, salt, pepper, and chili, stirring well. Add the vinegar, garlic, cumin, tomato, and a dash of soy sauce, and cook until onion is slightly limp. Add the reserved French fries. Stir, cooking until everything is warmed through. Remove from heat, and garnish with cilantro. Serve immediately with rice. Serves 4-6.

## Paradise Cafe
## 702 Anacapa Street, Santa Barbara
## 962-4416

The Paradise Cafe was once an Italian grocery and bakery, but most people remember it as La Paloma, the Mexican cafe that graced the corner of Anacapa and Ortega Streets for almost 50 years. I can remember sitting at the counter of La Paloma as a teenager, staring at the huge, romantic mural of the legend known as Flecha del Sol (Shooting at the Sun), and admiring my mother's enjoyment of the tripe in her menudo.

When Kevin Boss and Randy Rouse took over the cafe in the early 80's, they kept the mural, as well as the historical flavor of the old building. Even the name, Paradise, was chosen because it fit exactly into the original La Paloma neon sign.

The old cafe is now a lively, very popular bar and meeting place, while the adjacent restaurant is situated in the cottage where the owner used to live. The restaurant consists of two airy patios and two intimate dining rooms. I like to sit in the front room when it's flooded with the lingering late afternoon sun, but the wine-dark back room, with carpeting and brick walls, is also inviting.

The menu is simple and consistently good. You can always count on the freshness of the food from Paradise, along with its pleasant, efficient presentation. Its culinary influence might be traced to Santa Ynez regional cooking, with its oak wood barbecue tradition. The half dozen varieties of fresh fish that appear on the menu daily are succulently grilled on an oak grill, as are the generous hamburgers and steaks.

Along with its crunchy, fresh salads, the Paradise is famous for Huevos Valenzuela which Kevin and Randy have donated here. When they first bought the restaurant, they opened as a little breakfast place. One of their dishes was the Huevos Valenzuela, named in honor of Fernandez Valenzuela who was having his fabulous rookie year with the Dodgers at the time. The dish was so popular that their patrons demanded that they put it on the dinner menu.

## *HUEVOS VALENZUELA*

**8 eggs, scrambled**
**½ avocado, sliced**
**1-1½ cups Black Beans (recipe follows)**
**4 flour tortillas**
**½ cup Paradise Salsa (recipe follows)**
**¾ cup grated cheese, ½ cheddar and ½ jack**

Put ¼ of the eggs, avocado, and beans on each tortilla. Top with Salsa and roll up the tortilla. Place on a baking sheet, and cover the tops of the tortillas with cheese. Put under the broiler to melt the cheese, about 3-5 minutes. Serves 4.

## *Black Beans*

**½ pound dried black beans**
**1 bell pepper, chopped**
**½ Spanish onion, chopped**
**1 teaspoon chili powder (optional)**
**salt and pepper to taste**

Soak the beans overnight in a bowl of water. Drain off the water, and put the beans, bell pepper, onion, and spices in a large saucepan with a lid. With just enough water to cover, bring to a boil over high heat, then lower heat and simmer, covered, until beans are tender, about 2-3 hours. Stir occasionally, adding more water if needed. Makes 3 cups.

# *Paradise Salsa*

6 Italian plum tomatoes, chopped
½ bunch cilantro, chopped
3 green onions, chopped
½ jalapeno, minced
1 tablespoon red wine vinegar
salt to taste

Mix all the ingredients together well. Makes 1½ cups. Will last up to 5 days in the refrigerator.

# *COBB SALAD*

2 teaspoons Dijon mustard
2 tablespoons lemon juice
½ teaspoon sugar
salt and pepper to taste
¼ cup extra virgin olive oil
4 cups finely chopped lettuce (preferably the inner leaves)
1 cup chopped tomato
1 cup cooked diced chicken
1 cup cooked chopped bacon
1 cup chopped green onion
1 cup chopped avocado
4 hard boiled eggs, diced
1 cup crumbled blue cheese

In a small bowl, whisk together the mustard, lemon juice, sugar, salt, and pepper. Continue to whisk while pouring in the oil in a steady stream until dressing is thickened.

Mix together remaining ingredients in a large salad bowl. Toss with about half of the prepared dressing. Slowly add more dressing, to taste. Serves 4.

# *BLACK BEAN SOUP*

**1 pound dried black beans**
**2 cups chicken stock**
**chili powder to taste**
**salt and pepper to taste**
**sour cream and salsa for garnish**

Soak the beans overnight in a pot of water. Drain off the water, and place the beans in a large saucepan, with just enough water to cover. Bring to a boil over high heat, then turn down heat and simmer, covered, until beans are tender, about 2-3 hours. Stir occasionally, and add a bit more water if needed.

When beans are cooked, puree them in a food processor, using the pulse button. Do not over puree. Return to the pan, add the chicken stock, bring to a boil, and season to taste. Garnish with sour cream and salsa. Serves 6.

## Paul Bhalla's
## 1311 State Street, Santa Barbara
## 966-2733

My husband and I announced our engagement by sending out a photograph of him playing his sitar, while I accompanied him blissfully in the background on the tambura. We had discovered a love of India together, and for years anyone who came to our apartment for a party, came for curry and an Indian movie. Naturally, we go to Paul Bhalla's for all major romantic events.

Paul Bhalla was one of the first to open an Indian restaurant in Los Angeles in the early 70's. Now there are close to a hundred. So far, however, his is the only one in Santa Barbara. It's an excellent place to go for a taste of authentic Indian cuisine with its fantastic flavors and pungent spices.

Like a miniature museum display, the window on State Street, a few doors down from the Arlington, is filled with Indian treasures, hinting at the wonders within. The restaurant doesn't disappoint. Lit by dozens of brass lamps hanging from a stately, high ceiling, the chocolate brown walls are covered with old photographs and curios and prints from India, as well as an enormous tiger skin. I just love the atmosphere.

Besides the curries and the bhunas, many of the specialties at Paul Bhalla's are cooked in tandoori clay ovens. This is an ancient way of cooking that predates the microwave by several thousand years. After marinating the meat in yogurt and spices, it is lowered on skewers into the oven, where temperatures reach 1200 degrees. A chicken will cook in five minutes, and have a marvelous, succulent flavor. The wonderful breads are also baked in a matter of seconds by slapping them against the side of the oven, where they cook in just a few seconds. The recipe for Paratha given here however, can be made at home without a tandoori oven. At the restaurant it's called Tandoori Bread; I'm calling this version Fried Bread because it is made in a pan instead of an oven.

The entrees at Paul Bhalla's come with a number of condiments and chutneys as well sauces—raita made from yogurt and spices, and dahl made from lentils. (There are dozens of ways to make raita.) The fun of this food comes from the clusters of flavors you can get on your plate. Each bite is an adventure and no two bites taste quite the same.

With Indian food, I feel I have been granted an extraordinary pleasure that I might easily have missed in this life. I feel lucky to have sampled one of the great tastes of the world.

# RAITA

**2 cups plain yogurt**
**½ cup chopped onion**
**2 tablespoons chopped cilantro**
**¼ teaspoon red pepper**
**½ teaspoon cumin**
**1 cucumber, peeled and finely chopped**
**salt to taste**

Mix ingredients together. Serve as a relish with Shrimp Bhuna (recipe given) or any spicy food. Serves 6-8.

# SHRIMP BHUNA

½ cup plain yogurt
3 large cloves garlic, crushed
2 teaspoons ground cumin seed
3 teaspoons ground coriander
1 teaspoon salt
1 pound shrimp, peeled and deveined
3 tablespoons oil
1 cup onion, finely chopped
1 cup tomatoes, chopped
1 teaspoon ground cayenne
2 teaspoons paprika
1 lemon, cut in wedges
2 tablespoons chopped fresh cilantro

In a large bowl, put the yogurt, half the crushed garlic, 1 tea-spoon of the cumin, 1 teaspoon of the coriander, and salt. Mix well. Pat the shrimp dry, and add them to the yogurt mixture, making sure they are coated well. Marinate for 1-2 hours at room temperature.

In a heavy bottomed, large saucepan, put 2 tablespoons of the oil. Add the onions; fry on medium high heat, stirring constantly, until they are light brown, about 5 minutes. Add the tomatoes, and saute for another 2 minutes. Add the rest of the garlic, cumin, and coriander, along with the cayenne and paprika. Cook for 1 more minute; the sauce should not be runny. If so, cook a little longer. Remove from heat and set aside.

Using the same pan, heat the remaining 1 tablespoon of oil on high heat. Do not let it burn or smoke. Add the marinated shrimp, and cook, stirring constantly, for 2 minutes. The pan should be sizzling. Add the sauce back into the pan, and con-tinue cooking for 2 minutes, or until the shrimp are cooked. Do not overcook. Remove from heat and serve immediately. Garnish with lemon wedges and cilantro. Serves 4.

# *PARATHA*
# *(FRIED BREAD)*

**2 cups whole wheat flour**
**6 tablespoons ghee (see note) or vegetable oil**
**½-1 cup cold water**

Mix the flour and 2 tablespoons of ghee together in a bowl. The mixture will be crumbly. Add ½ cup of water to the mixture, and knead to make a soft dough. If the dough falls apart, add a little more water. Kneed until smooth and elastic. Cover with a cloth and let sit for ½ hour.

Divide the dough into 8 pieces. Take each piece and roll it out with a rolling pin into a 7-inch circle. Brush some ghee on top of the dough and fold it in half. Brush more ghee on top and fold again. Then roll out the dough again, to form a circle or triangle. Repeat this procedure 8 times, and then cover the dough with a damp cloth until ready to fry.

To cook, heat a thin layer of oil in a frying pan until very hot and fry until crisp and evenly browned. Spread more ghee on top if desired. Keep warm until ready to serve. Serves 8.

Note: Ghee is a clarified butter that has been taken one step further. It has a nutty flavor and will keep for months. Take ½ pound unsalted butter, and melt it slowly in a heavy saucepan. Bring it to a boil, stir briefly, then reduce the heat as low as possible. Simmer, undisturbed and uncovered, for 45 minutes. Strain the ghee through several layers of dampened cheesecloth. If any remnants of butter solids remain, strain it again.

# Pavlako's

## Pavlako's
### 217 North Milpas Street, Santa Barbara
### 965-6203

Pavlako's is the only restaurant in town that takes up an entire city block—albeit a small, triangular shaped block perched right on Milpas Street. There's just enough room on the sidewalk out in front, under two beautiful, lush trees, for the breakfast crowd to wait cheerfully for their turn at a table.

I once overheard a woman telling a friend that she was going to Utah "to find a man." I would recommend going to Pavlako's early in the morning. It's filled with just the kind of men she was looking for.

Pavlako's was started in 1979 by Paul Brown and his two sons, Chris and Nick. Chris and his wife, Pamela, now own the restaurant. Although it pays tribute to the family's Greek origins, Pavlako's isn't really a Greek restaurant. Rather, it's an all-American diner, bustling with big breakfasts, sociable lunches, cozy dinners, and warm camaraderie. It has a raised counter with stools, a lot of little wooden tables, and plenty to keep your eyes busy.

Some of the dishes, however, are Greek, and this is one of the things that makes Pavlako's special. The eatery is famous for its Greek eggs, which combine eggs with Feta cheese and vegetables. Their Greek Village Salad is a classic, and it's a lucky night that features the Avgolemono Soup. I've managed to get Chris to share both of them.

I almost made Pavlako's nationally famous. I was having breakfast there one morning when I got a call asking me to be an extra on the soap opera, "Santa Barbara." (Honest.) I planned to say in my bio that I got discovered at the counter at Pavlako's. Alas, despite my entirely new wardrobe, I didn't even go before the cameras. Pavlako's will just have to settle for being famous as the favorite eatery for lots of happy patrons.

# DOLMADES
# (STUFFED GRAPE LEAVES)

**1½ pounds ground beef or lamb**
**1 egg**
**1 onion, finely chopped**
**1 clove garlic, chopped**
**3 tablespoons tomato paste**
**½ bunch Italian parsley, chopped**
**½ cup uncooked rice**
**5 tablespoons olive oil, dived usage**
**¼ cup sherry**
**2-3 teaspoons oregano**
**1-2 tablespoons water**
**dash of nutmeg**
**dash of cinnamon**
**salt and pepper to taste**
**ᵉᵒ grapes leaves, (approximately, can used canned), rinsed**
    **and drained**
**1 cup chicken broth**

Combine all the ingredients, except the grape leaves, chicken broth, and 2 tablespoons of the olive oil. Mix well.

To stuff the leaves, lay them out with the stem pointing up. Use two leaves if they are little. Place a small amount of filling near the stem. Roll up, folding the sides in.

Line the bottom of a saucepan with a layer of grape leaves. Place the stuffed leaves in the pot, folded side down. Add chicken broth, reserved olive oil, and just enough water to cover. Place a heavy plate on top of the dolmades to prevent them from floating. Cover the pot, and simmer for 1 hour. Let stand for at least 1 hour. Serve hot or cold. Makes 2-3 dozen.

## VILLAGE SALAD

**1 cucumber, sliced and peeled**
**1 large tomato, cut in wedges**
**½ cup crumbled feta cheese**
**½ red onion, sliced**
**16 Greek olives**
**ground black pepper to taste**
**lemon pepper to taste**
**dried oregano to taste**
**3-4 tablespoons olive oil**

Arrange the cucumber slices, tomato wedges, onion, and olives on 4 plates. Top with feta cheese. Sprinkle with the herbs and peppers, and pour olive oil over the top. Serves 4.

## AVGOLEMONO SOUP

**4 cups chicken broth**
**salt and pepper to taste**
**¼ cup orzo noodles**
**2 eggs**
**juice of 1-2 lemons**

Bring the broth to a boil. Add salt and pepper to taste. Add the orzo. Simmer until the orzo is "al dente," according to package directions.
Beat the eggs until they are frothy. Add ½ cup of the broth to the eggs, stirring constantly to avoid lumps. Slowly pour the eggs into the broth. Add the lemon juice, and correct seasoning. Serves 4.

## Pierre Lafond
## 516 San Ysidro Road, Montecito
## 565-1502

You hear it all the time. How for years some child ate nothing but peanut butter sandwiches. My son, Ted, is one of those kids—with one big difference. His food of choice is Pierre Lafond's turkey sandwiches (sourdough, no tomato). He'd eat them three times a day if he could. I don't mind taking him there. The place is never boring. In fact, the food and shopping options are kaleidoscopic, from blueberry vinegar to candied kiwi slices. Where else can you stop for a sandwich and get a new sweater, pick up a cup of coffee and look at a canopy bed, or select a fresh salad and new set of dishes?

Pierre Lafond started out almost 30 years ago as a small liquor store that sold a few gifts. Today, its deli, bakery, and wine store are flanked by two clothing stores and an eclectic housewares/gift shop. The deli also has a branch on the Mesa.

Lafond and his wife, Wendy Foster, turn the phrase "What's new?" into an everyday reality. The merchandise, the layout, and the food changes constantly, always seemingly for the better. They make the store as interesting to visit as the clientele are fun to watch. (This the best people watching place in Santa Barbara.)

You can run into the deli and grab a cup of coffee—brewed fresh from their selection of 38 varieties of beans. Or you can get caught up in a leisurely perusal of taste bud fantasies. The deli boasts 20 kinds of mustard on shelves filled with imported and gourmet items. Wines, party supplies, cards, handmade chocolates, coffees, teas, and food-to-go make this the perfect place for picnic and gift baskets.

Besides sandwiches, the deli prepares homemade dishes like chili relleno pie, vegetarian lasagna, enchiladas, and avocados stuffed with crab salad. The bakery produces fresh muffins, brownies, scones, lemon bars, and their famous Giant Chocolate Chip Cookies included here, which are so delicious Ted won't even give me a single bite.

The deli has my choice for the best salad bar in Santa Barbara. It makes dieting a privilege. It has homemade dressings and a selection of more than 30 vegetables, fruits, and mixed salads to go on top of spinach or lettuce. Ted likes the baby corn and hearts of palm. I go for the Corn Fiesta, the guacamole and the artichoke hearts. We both love the Dijon Vinaigrette Dressing. Together, we have quite a nice little feast. We eat outdoors in the sunshine near the blue reflecting pool. After school snacks have come a long way.

# DIJON VINAIGRETTE SALAD DRESSING

**1 clove garlic**
**1 teaspoon dill**
**1 teaspoon tarragon**
**1 teaspoon parsley**
**¼ teaspoon salt**
**¼ teaspoon pepper**
**2 tablespoons Dijon mustard**
**¼ cup rice wine vinegar**
**1 cup olive oil**

Drop the garlic into a food processor, using the chopping blade. Add all the remaining ingredients, and process until smooth. Makes 1 1/3 cups.

# CORN FIESTA

6 cups drained canned corn
½ pound mozzarella
1 green bell pepper, diced
2 tomatoes, diced
½ red onion, diced
½ bunch green onions, chopped
1 small jar pimientos
1 clove garlic
¼ cup red wine vinegar
¾ cup cottonseed oil
1½ teaspoons salt
1½ teaspoons cumin
1 tablespoon chili powder
¼ teaspoon cayenne

Slice the cheese into chunks that are ¼ inch square. Add the bell pepper, tomatoes, red onion, and green onion. Drain and rinse the pimientos. Toss all the ingredients together in a large bowl.

Chop the garlic in a food processor, and then add all the remaining ingredients, and blend. Pour over the salad and toss again. Makes 1- 1-cup servings.

# SZECHWAN PASTA

1 package angel hair pasta, 12-16 ounces
1/8 pound snow peas
1 cup mayonnaise
1/3 cup soy sauce
1 tablespoon chili oil
1/8 cup sesame oil
1½ teaspoons Dijon mustard
1 clove garlic
¼ pound cooked turkey, diced
½ bunch green onions, chopped
1 medium carrot, diced

½ can water chestnuts, drained and sliced
1 red bell pepper, diced
½ cup sliced baby corn on the cob
½ bunch cilantro leaves, chopped
2 tablespoons toasted sesame seeds

Cook the angel hair pasta until al dente, according to package directions. Drain, rinse with cold water to avoid sticking and drain again. Pull stringy stems off snow peas, and slice on the diagonal into thin strips.

Combine the mayonnaise, soy sauce, chili oil, sesame oil, Dijon mustard, and garlic in a food processor or blender.

Combine the pasta, snow peas, turkey, green onions, carrot, water chestnuts, bell pepper, and baby corn in a large bowl. Pour on the mayonnaise dressing to taste, and toss well. Garnish with sesame seeds and cilantro. Serves 4-6.

# GIANT CHOCOLATE CHIP COOKIES

½ pound unsalted butter
1 cup sugar
1 cup brown sugar
2 eggs
2 teaspoons vanilla
1 teaspoon salt
1 teaspoon baking soda
2½ cups flour
2 cups chocolate chips

Preheat the oven to 325 degrees. In a large bowl, cream the butter and both sugars together. Add the eggs and mix well. Add all the remaining ingredients except the chocolate chips and mix until combined. Be careful not to over mix. Add the chocolate chips.

Lightly grease a pair of cookie sheets. Using a spoon or scoop, scoop a generous amount of dough (approximately ¼ cup) for each cookie. Be sure to place the dough 3-4 inches apart on the cookie sheet because the dough will spread while baking. Bake for 15-20 minutes. Let cool before serving. Makes 2 dozen.

## Restaurant Mimosa
## 2700 De La Vina Street, Santa Barbara
## 682-2465

When I saw the astonishing and mouth watering "Babette's Feast," the movie about a once-in-a-lifetime meal, I was left, not surprisingly, with a hunger for great food. So where did we go to eat after Babette's feast? Restaurant Mimosa, in honor of its French chef, and we made the right choice.

Chef Camille Schwartz, who began his training in Paris at the age of 15, has cooked all over the world. He came to Santa Barbara in 1977, introducing his wonderful French cuisine at the San Ysidro Ranch. Six years later, he and his wife, Anne, opened Restaurant Mimosa.

The restaurant has the feeling of an elegant, French Provincial manor, decorated in floral wallpaper and pale greens. Airy lattice-work divides the restaurant into intimate eating areas, and the lattice pattern is pleasingly replicated in the elegant china. This is the kind of place you want to take your parents to, in order to show them what a wonderful son or daughter you turned out to be. They will decide you are subtle, complex, and brilliant, even though it's really the cuisine.

The restaurant is noted for its game dishes that include quail, rabbit, and wild pigeon. Regular customers often arrange their visits to coincide with the Mimosa sweetbreads, which are prepared in a variety of ways. When Chef Schwartz gave me this recipe for sweetbreads, prepared with white mushrooms, spinach, cognac, and cream, he named them "Veal Sweetbread Babette" in honor of the compliment I had paid him by going there after the movie.

# *LENTIL AND VEGETABLE CURRY SOUP*

**1 cup lentils**
**3 teaspoons vegetable oil**
**½ cup chopped celery**
**½ cup chopped carrots**
**½ cup chopped onions**
**4 cups chicken stock**
**1 teaspoon curry powder**
**salt and pepper to taste**

Wash lentils and cover them with water for about half an hour, then strain them. In the meantime, place the oil in a soup pot over medium high heat and add the vegetables. Cook for 5 minutes, stirring occasionally. Add the chicken stock, curry powder, and salt and pepper to taste. Bring to a boil, add the lentils, and when soup begins to boil again, lower heat and let simmer for 15 minutes, or until lentils are done. Serves 6-8.

# VEAL ROQUEFORT

**2 tablespoons oil, approximately**
**2 tablespoons butter, approximately**
**1 large stalk celery, chopped**
**1 large carrot, chopped**
**½ medium onion, chopped**
**salt and black ground pepper**
**1 cup water**
**3 ounces Roquefort cheese**
**1½ pounds veal**
**flour for coating veal**
**1 cup heavy cream**
**1/3 cup finely chopped parsley**

Put 1 teaspoon of oil and 1 teaspoon butter in a small saucepan over medium high heat. Add the celery, carrots, and onions and saute until golden brown. Then add salt and pepper, and cover with 1 cup of water. Bring to a boil, lower heat and let simmer again until the vegetables are tender. Remove from heat and puree the vegetables in a blender. Add the Roquefort cheese, blending until smooth.

Cut the veal into approximately 18 scallopini and pound well. Using a 10-inch saute pan, add enough oil and butter to cover the bottom of the pan. Dip the veal scallopini lightly in the flour, add a little salt and pepper, and saute in the pan over very high heat for 15 seconds on each side. Place as many scallopini as will comfortably fit in the pan. Remove and keep warm. When all the veal is done, discard the grease, and put the heavy cream and vegetable-Roquefort mixture in the pan. Add the chopped parsley. Let simmer for a few minutes, until the cream is heated through. Check the seasonings, then pour over the veal.
Serves 6.

# BOUILLABAISSE

¼ cup olive oil
1 medium carrot, cut into 2-inch thin sticks
1 small onion, chopped
1 celery stalk, cut into 2-inch thin sticks
1 small leek, cut into 2-inch thin sticks
1 ounce garlic, chopped
2 medium potatoes, diced small
3 cups fish stock or water
1 large tomato, diced
3 ounces tomato puree
pinch of saffron
6 to 8 fresh basil leaves, sliced thin
¼ teaspoon fennel seeds
1/6 teaspoon whole thyme
1 teaspoon parsley, chopped
salt and black ground pepper to taste
3 pounds assorted seafood, such as sea bass, halibut, salmon,
    orange roughy, prawns, scallops, lobster, cut into small
    chunks
24 mussels or 18 clams
garlic croutons for garnish

Put a large stewpot over medium high heat, and add the olive
oil, carrot, onion, celery, leek, garlic, and potatoes. Saute for 5
minutes, then add the fish stock or water. Add the diced tomatoes, tomato puree, saffron, basil, fennel, thyme, parsley, salt,
and pepper. Bring to a boil, and then lower heat and let simmer
for 5 minutes. Add the fish. Bring to a boil for 3 minutes, then
add shellfish. When the mussels or clams open, the soup is
ready. Correct seasonings and use garlic croutons for garnish.
Serves 6.

# *VEAL SWEETBREAD BABETTE*

1 carrot, cut into 1-inch sticks
½ celery stalk, cut into 1-inch sticks
¼ onion, sliced thinly
pinch of fresh thyme
salt and pepper to taste
6 cups water
2½-3 pounds veal sweetbreads, soaked in cold water for at
    least 1 hour, changing water 2-3 times
3 ounces butter
½ pound white mushrooms, sliced
1½ cups heavy cream
¼ cup brandy
1 bunch fresh spinach, washed and dried
1 bunch chives, cut finely

Place the carrot, celery, onion, thyme, salt, and pepper in a soup
pot with the 6 cups of water over high heat. Bring to a boil and
let boil for 5 minutes. Add the sweetbreads. Make sure that the
liquid covers everything; if not, add more water. Bring to a boil,
lower heat, and simmer for 20 minutes. Remove the sweetbreads
and immerse them in cold water. Discard the cooking liquid.
When sweetbreads are cool, drain them and clean by removing
cartilage, connective tissue and tough membranes. Cut into
1-inch cubes.

Using a big saute pan, heat the butter. When hot, saute the
sweetbreads with the mushrooms. When they are slightly brown,
add the brandy, cream, salt, and pepper, and let simmer for 5
minutes.

Spread spinach leaves onto 6 warm plates and put the sweetbreads over the spinach. Sprinkle with chives. Serves 6.

## The Shoals at the Cliff House
### 6602 W. Pacific Coast Highway, Mussels Shoals
### 684-0025

Perched on a bluff between the highway and the ocean half way to Ventura, the Cliff House has been in existence since 1947. It's a wonderful piece of Americana, with a delightfully garish neon sign. It was called a motel for years, but it is now a very romantic inn.

I had always wanted to stop there, especially after I started hearing good things about the new restaurant. I finally made the trip to the Shoals for dinner, and I'm only sorry I didn't go sooner. The ride out with a couple of friends seemed to take five minutes instead of 20. It was enlivened that night by the waves crashing right up onto the freeway. But when we got to the Shoals, it wasn't inundated with salt water, as I had feared. The Cliff House actually sits securely on a fabulous bluff overlooking the ocean. What a magic spot.

The restaurant is classy but unpretentious, situated on the ground floor of the three story inn. Green table cloths, wrought iron chairs with shell-shaped backs, and lots of plants give the restaurant a garden feeling. The view from the window tables is spectacular, but on a cool night, the restaurant is so cozy you can't even hear the waves. On more balmy nights, dinners are served at tables on the patio overlooking paradise.

In the two years the Shoals has been open, they have put a lot of variety into their dinners. They prepare a new menu every week.

The selection is limited to three appetizers and six or seven entrees. I like this. Too long a menu tends to make me nervous. Manager Sanford Porter says that he and chef Douglas Russell put a call out to the fishing boats before deciding on the menu. When the Shoals says fresh, they mean it. The menu also has chicken, steak, and pasta dishes.

Russell created all of the recipes here except the Baked Papaya. This was created by Michele Porter, Sanford's sister and co-manager of the Shoals. The recipe was the winner of the national Uncle Ben's Rice "Inn to Inn" recipe contest.

## BROILED AHI SALAD WITH SOY RICE VINAIGRETTE

**18 ounces ahi tuna, sliced**
**1 head romaine lettuce**
**1 head red leaf lettuce**
**1 carrot, shredded**
**¼ head red cabbage, shredded**
**½ cup white wine**
**½ cup rice vinegar**
**¼ cup soy sauce**
**1 tablespoon chopped garlic**
**1 tablespoon chopped shallots**
**1 teaspoon black pepper**
**1 scallion, diced**
**3 Roma tomatoes, sliced**

Broil the ahi on the barbecue or in the broiler for 30 seconds on each side. Set aside.

Break up the lettuce, and toss with the shredded carrot and cabbage in a large bowl. Combine wine, vinegar, soy sauce, garlic, shallots, and pepper in a small bowl. Drizzle onto salad ingredients and toss. Divide the salad onto 6 plates. Place the broiled ahi on top of the salad. Garnish with scallions and tomatoes. Serve 6.

# SPINACH AND RICOTTA CHEESE CANAPE

**1½ pounds spinach, washed and coarsely chopped**
**1 pound ricotta cheese**
**2 teaspoons chopped garlic**
**1 egg, beaten**
**½ teaspoon salt**
**½ teaspoon pepper**
**¼ pound puff pastry sheet (store bought or homemade)**

Preheat oven to 425 degrees. Mix the spinach, cheese, garlic, eggs, salt, and pepper together in a large bowl. Line the pastry sheet with the spinach mixture. Roll up the pastry dough, folding the edges in on the last roll.

Bake at 425 degrees for 20 minutes, or until golden brown. Let cool; slice and serve. Serves 6.


# BAKED PAPAYA UNCLE BEN'S

**2 cups ricotta cheese**
**½ cup mango chutney, chopped**
**1 tablespoon curry powder**
**½ cup thinly sliced green onions**
**½ cup raisins**
**3 cups cooked Uncle Ben's rice (cooked according to package instructions)**
**6 papayas**
**¼ cup sugar**
**1 teaspoon cinnamon**
**½ cup melted butter**

Preheat the oven to 450 degrees. In a bowl, mix the ricotta cheese, chutney, and curry until smooth. Fold in the green onions, raisins, and cooked rice.

Cut 6 papayas in half and remove seeds. Fill the centers with the rice mixture. Combine sugar and cinnamon together, and sprinkle on top. Drizzle with melted butter.

Bake about 15 minutes, until heated through. Serve immediately. Serves 12.

# BLACKENED CHICKEN WITH PECAN BUTTER SAUCE

**Blackened spices:**
>    **1 tablespoon black pepper**
>    **1 tablespoon white pepper**
>    **1 tablespoon cayenne pepper**
>    **1 tablespoon fennel seed**
>    **1 tablespoon dried thyme**
>    **1 tablespoon dried, sweet basil**
>    **1 tablespoon salt**

**6 boneless chicken breast halves**
**Pecan Butter Sauce (recipe follows)**

Mix the blackened spices together. Roll the chicken in the spices, pressing them into the meat. Broil the chicken, until it is almost but not quite cooked through, about 5 minutes per side (chicken will continue cooking while you prepare sauce). Set aside, and prepare Pecan Butter Sauce. Slice and fan the chicken on a plate, cover with sauce, and serve. Serves 6.

## *Pecan Butter Sauce*

**½ cup white wine**
**4 tablespoons lemon juice**
**1 tablespoon shallots**
**3 tablespoons cream**
**½ pound sweet butter**
**salt and white pepper to taste**
**4 tablespoons chopped pecans**

In a saucepan, combine the wine, lemon juice, and shallots. Bring to a boil over high heat and reduce liquid down to one quarter. Add the cream, and reduce by half. Turn the heat down, and add the sweet butter, a little at a time, using a wire whisk. Take off the heat. Add salt, pepper, and the chopped pecans. Makes about ½ cup.

# BROILED LAMB LOIN WITH ROASTED GARLIC, OYSTER MUSHROOM AND GREEN PEPPERCORN SAUCE

**6 heads garlic**
**6 boneless lamb loins, 8 ounces each**
**Oyster Mushroom and Green Peppercorn Sauce (recipe follows)**

Preheat the oven to 450 degrees. Roast the 6 heads of garlic in the oven for 10-12 minutes. Set aside.

Broil the lamb to your taste (7 minutes a side for rare), and set aside. Make the Mushroom Peppercorn Sauce.

Take the roasted garlic, cut the papery tops off, and place on 6 plates. Slice the lamb and fan out slices on the plates. Spoon sauce over the lamb, and serve. Serves 6.

## Oyster Mushroom and Green Peppercorn Sauce

**½ stick butter**
**1 tablespoon chopped shallots**
**1 teaspoon green peppercorns**
**¼ pound oyster mushrooms, sliced**
**1 cup beef or chicken stock**
**1 cup cream**
**1 teaspoon minced garlic**
**1 teaspoon lemon thyme**

In a saute pan, heat the butter, shallots, and green peppercorns. Saute over medium high heat for 1 minute. Add the mushrooms and stock, bring to a boil and reduce liquid by half. Add the cream, garlic, lemon thyme, salt, and pepper. Reduce liquid by half, and remove from heat. Makes about 1 cup.

## Shores of Siam
### 2829 De La Vina Street, Santa Barbara
### 687-8146

One of my friends knows a Thai translator who says that the Shores of Siam is the most authentic of all the Thai restaurants in Santa Barbara. Not that I could tell from authentic. I just love Thai food—the sweet, the spice, and the surprise of it all.

The Shores of Siam was recently remodelled, replacing dark wood panelling with white walls, celestial blue trim, and lace curtains. A substantial new patio has been built, and the two dining rooms of the restaurant are now divided by an enormous fish tank, one of several in the restaurant.

Owner/chef Buntoon Boonyagarn, whose friends call him Toon, used to cook for the Prince of Thailand. He has been in this country for 20 years, and says he opened the very first Thai restaurant in San Francisco 17 years ago. In 1985 he opened the Shores of Siam.

Buntoon and his partner, Cindy Boonyagarn, grow their own lemon grass, basil mint and fresh galanga, a member of the ginger family used to flavor the wonderful Tom Ka Gai (Chicken Coconut Soup) explained here. This soup, a light coconut chicken broth, filled with chunks of chicken and mushrooms, with a lemony flavor and a hint of spice, is one of my favorites; and the Shores of Siam does it to savory perfection.

Toon also shares two of the great favorites at his restaurant: Kang Keo Wan Gai (Green Curry Chicken) and Seafood Pad Thai, a dish of noodles with chicken, shrimp, scallops, green onions, vegetables, ground peanuts, and cilantro. Both of these recipes contain that magic meld of flavors that is the hallmark of Thai cooking. If chefs like Buntoon hadn't brought their cooking to California, we might have all moved to Thailand by now.

# *TOM KA GAI*
# *(CHICKEN COCONUT SOUP)*

**1½ cups chicken broth**
**1 cup diced chicken**
**3 tablespoons lemon juice**
**2 slices galanga (Thai ginger, available at Asian markets)**
**3 tablespoons fish sauce (available at Asian markets)**
**1 teaspoon Thai chili paste (available at Asian markets)**
**½ stalk lemon grass, sliced at an angle into 1-inch pieces**
  **(available at Asian markets)**
**1 tablespoon sugar**
**1/8 cup straw mushrooms**
**1 can (12 ounces) coconut milk**
**1 green onion, diced**
**¼ cup sliced white mushrooms**
**fresh chopped cilantro, to taste**

Bring the chicken broth to a boil in a soup pot. Add the chicken, lemon juice, galanga, fish sauce, chili paste, lemon grass, sugar, and straw mushrooms. Bring to a boil, lower heat, and simmer for 5 minutes.

Add the coconut milk, and bring to a boil. In a serving bowl, place the green onions, white mushrooms, and cilantro. Pour the hot soup into the bowl, and serve. Serves 4.

# KANG KEO WAN GAI
# (GREEN CURRY CHICKEN)

1 tablespoon vegetable oil
1 tablespoon green curry paste (Kang Keo Wan in Asian markets)
2 cups thinly sliced, skinless chicken breast
2 tablespoons fish sauce (available at Asian markets)
1 tablespoon sugar
2 cups coconut milk
½ cup frozen green peas
1 cup sliced fresh zucchini
½ cup sliced green bell pepper
steamed rice

Heat the oil in a sauce pan over medium high heat, and add the green curry paste. Stir until the paste is dissolved. Add the chicken, fish sauce, and sugar, and continue to stir until the chicken is cooked.

Add the coconut milk; let simmer at a low boil for 5 minutes. Add the peas, zucchini, and green bell peppers; stir until the zucchini is cooked—2-3 minutes. Serve over steamed rice. Serves 4.

# SEAFOOD PAD THAI
# (SEAFOOD NOODLES)

1 pound Thai rice noodles (available at Asian markets)
¼ cup vegetable oil
1 tablespoon minced garlic
1 cup diced tofu
12 shrimp, cleaned and peeled
12 scallops
1 cup sliced chicken breasts
2 eggs, beaten
2 tablespoons fish sauce (available at Asian markets)
3 tablespoons lime or lemon juice

**2 tablespoons dried turnip (available at Asian markets, optional)**
**2 tablespoons ground dried shrimp**
**2 tablespoons sugar**
**1 tablespoon paprika**
**2 cups mung bean sprouts**
**1 cup green onions, sliced in one-inch pieces**
**1½ tablespoons minced peanuts for garnish**
**¼ cup chopped cilantro for garnish**
**½ cup grated carrots for garnish**
**lime wedges for garnish**

Soak the noodles in warm water, and put aside. In a large skillet, heat the oil over high heat, and brown the garlic and tofu. Add the shrimp, scallops, and chicken. Saute until cooked, stirring constantly. Add the eggs and continue stirring.

Drain the noodles, and add to the skillet, stirring well. Continue cooking, and add the fish sauce, lime juice, turnip, dried shrimp, sugar, and paprika. Stir well. Add the sprouts and green onion, and stir until the sprouts are cooked, but not soft. Serve on a large platter. Garnish with peanuts, cilantro, grated carrots, and wedges of lime. Serves 4.

# PAD KING KAI (GINGER CHICKEN)

**4 skinless and boneless chicken breast halves**
**1/8 cup vegetable oil**
**½ cup fresh ginger, sliced in thin narrow strips**
**1 cup sliced green bell pepper**
**1 cup sliced onions**
**1 cup sliced green onions**
**1 tablespoon fish sauce (available at Asian markets)**
**1 teaspoon sugar**
**1 teaspoon minced garlic**
**½ teaspoon black pepper**
**½ teaspoon sesame oil**
**½ teaspoon soy sauce**

Slice the chicken into thin strips, and saute it in oil over medium high heat. Add the ginger, and cook for 5 minutes, stirring constantly.

Add the remaining ingredients, and saute until the onions are tender. (If the ingredients become dry while cooking, add approximately 1/8 cup of water.) Serves 4.

Note: 1 pound of beef or pork may be substituted for the chicken.

## STICKY RICE WITH MANGO AND SESAME SEEDS

**2 cups sticky rice (available at Asian markets)**
**1 teaspoon salt**
**½ cup sugar**
**1¼ cups coconut milk**
**4 ripe mangoes**
**2 teaspoons toasted sesame seeds**

Soak the rice in water for 4-6 hours. Wrap the soaked rice in cheese cloth, and place in a steamer with 2-3 inches of water on the bottom. (If you do not have a steamer pot, use a vegetable steamer placed inside of a deep pan that has a tight-fitting lid. Fill the pot with water, up to but not touching the vegetable steamer. Place the cheese cloth-wrapped rice on the vegetable steamer, and cover the pan with the lid.) Cook for 25-30 minutes. When the rice is done, it will feel soft and sticky.

In a mixing bowl, dissolve the salt and sugar into 1 cup of coconut milk. Add the cooked sticky rice, and stir until well blended. Cover and let stand for 10 minutes.

Peel the mangoes, slice them, and then refrigerate them for 10 minutes. In a small saucepan, slowly heat the remaining ¼ cup of coconut milk.

Mound the sticky rice onto the center of a serving plate, pour the heated coconut milk on top, and sprinkle with toasted sesame seeds. Arrange the sliced mangoes around the edge of the plate and serve. Serves 4-6 as a dessert.

## Soho
## 21 West Victoria Street, Santa Barbara
## 965-5497

"There's a Soho in London and a Soho in New York, so why not Santa Barbara?" asked Nancy Weiss. This young woman, formerly the chef at Zelo's, has both vision and spunk. She set up her Soho restaurant next to the Victoria Street Theater at the beginning of 1988, and people have been flocking to it ever since.

Hip, elegant, and different, it has been aptly called the Soho Food Gallery because it provides a constantly changing exhibition not only of the art on the walls, but of Weiss's cooking.

Whether you visit the restaurant in the clear, rosy light of day or the sophisticated hours of the evening, you will be treated to the imaginative, ethnic-flavored cuisine of an original cook who is full of surprises. Sweet Potato Jalapeno Soup and Greek Lemon Chicken Salad are two examples featured here of her inspired way with ingredients and flavors.

Another innovative touch to Soho is the way it caters to the odd hour eaters among us. A daily list of appetizer/specials is served late into the afternoon and long into the evening (until midnight), hours when fine dining is almost unattainable elsewhere in Santa Barbara. Smaller in portion as well as price, than the entrees, these specials sometimes include the Soft Blue Corn Tacos with Lime Grilled

Chicken. They change frequently, allowing Weiss further experimentation with her love of cooking.

The long, narrow, and freshly remodeled restaurant is divided into four dining areas. There is also a counter that looks into the kitchen. I suspect it's there because Weiss likes to see who her patrons are. She encourages custom orders—no cream, no salt, or whatever. She's an artist who cares about her public.

# SWEET POTATO JALAPENO SOUP

**4 medium sweet potatoes**
**1 tablespoon butter**
**1 large onion, diced**
**2 teaspoons salt**
**1 teaspoon pepper**
**6 cups chicken or vegetable stock**
**2 jalapenos, seeded and minced**
**1 cup heavy cream**

Bake the sweet potatoes until soft. When cool, peel and slice them. Set aside.

Melt the butter over medium high heat in a saucepan, and add the onions, salt, and pepper. Saute until onions are soft. In a food processor or blender, blend the potatoes with the onions. Add the stock and blend. Return soup to saucepan. Add the jalapenos and cream, and heat gently. Serves 4.

# GREEK LEMON CHICKEN SALAD

**6 boneless, skinless chicken breast halves**
**2 bunches spinach, washed and dried**
**1 red onion, thinly sliced**
**¼ pound sun dried tomatoes in oil, drained and slivered**
**½ cup Greek olives, green or black**
**12 cooked artichoke hearts (fresh, frozen or canned)**
**1 cucumber, peeled and sliced**
**3 tablespoons capers**
**¼ pound crumbled Feta cheese**
**¼ pound shelled pistachios**
**Lemon Vinaigrette (recipe follows)**

Poach the chicken breasts, cool, and dice them. Layer the spinach on 6 individual plates. Arrange the rest of the ingredients on top, and pour on Lemon Vinaigrette. (The dressing can also be served on the side.) Serves 6.

## *Lemon Vinaigrette*

**1 egg**
**¼ cup lemon juice**
**¼ cup rice wine vinegar**
**1/8 teaspoon celery seed**
**¼ teaspoon Greek oregano**
**salt and pepper to taste**
**1 tablespoon sugar**
**1 cup good olive oil**

Whisk the egg with all the ingredients except the olive oil. Emulsify the dressing by adding the olive oil in a slow, steady stream, while beating continuously. Makes about 1½ cups.

# SOFT BLUE CORN TACOS WITH LIME GRILLED CHICKEN

½ onion, cut in half
1 bunch cilantro
¼ cup lime juice
6 tablespoons brown sugar
salt and pepper
½ jalapeno, seeded
½ cup peanut oil
4 whole boneless skinless chicken breasts
Blue Corn Tortillas (recipe follows)
salsa to taste

Combine the onion, cilantro, lime juice, brown sugar, salt, pepper, jalapeno, and peanut oil in a food processor or blender. Pour over chicken breasts, cover, and marinate overnight in the refrigerator, turning occasionally.

The next day, make the Blue Corn Tortillas. Grill the chicken over hot coals until done. Cut into strips and roll strips in warmed tortillas. Serve with salsa. Serves 6.

## Blue Corn Tortillas

2 cups salted water
4 tablespoons butter
2 cups blue corn meal
3 cups all purpose flour

In a large saucepan, bring the water to a boil with the butter. Add the blue corn meal, whisk, and cook for 5 minutes. Let mixture cool completely, then knead with the flour. Form dough into balls that are 2 inches in diameter, and press between wax paper until flat. Cook on a lightly oiled griddle until browned. Keep warm until ready to serve. Makes 12 tortillas.

# AMARETTO POACHED PEARS WITH VANILLA CREAM

**4 firm, full-flavored pears**
**1 cup amaretto**
**1 cup water**
**1/8 cup sugar**
**1 cinnamon stick**
**3 whole cloves**
**1 cup heavy cream**
**1 teaspoon vanilla**

Peel the pears, cut them in half, and seed them. In a large saucepan, bring to a boil the pears, amaretto, water, sugar, cinnamon, and cloves. Lower heat slightly, and boil until pears are soft. Remove the pears. Continue boiling the liquid until it is reduced to a syrup.

Meanwhile, add the vanilla to the cream, and chill it until it is very cold. Swirl the cream into the syrup, and serve it on the pears. Serves 4.

## The Sojourner Coffee House
## 134 East Canon Perdido Street, Santa Barbara
## 965-7922

Both a coffeehouse and a restaurant, the Sojourner, or "the Soj" as it's affectionately called, has built up a very loyal clientele in the ten years it's been open.

It's always been one of my favorite restaurants in Santa Barbara. I find it cozy, predictable, and relaxing. With its paneling of light wood, soft lighting, and background hum of muted jazz and lively conversations, it feels like the living room of a dear old friend.

It started out as a coffeehouse, gradually adding dishes along vegetarian lines. Two of its most popular dishes are Vegetarian Lasagna and Baked Potato Supreme, a hot potato overflowing with assorted vegetables like broccoli and cauliflower, with garlic butter, and melted jack and cheddar cheeses. Of the recipes given here, the Gypsy Lentil Soup and the Apple Crisp are both all-time favorites.

The menu also includes a few chicken and fish dishes, lots of salads, and a great variety of drinks from cappuccino and hot fruit wine to the Sojo Smoothie and the Mocha Frosted.

The restaurant was badly damaged by a fire in 1988. After closing for several months, it reopened, a little more polished, but essentially the same. The Sojourner displays the work of local artists and also has a pretty decent community bulletin board. And they have a great view of the of the new/old Presidio across the street.

Owner Wally Marantette says that his restaurant doesn't depend on tourists for trade. He likes that. "I enjoy seeing the same faces and getting to know people. You can't beat the consistency. We're as busy in the dead of winter as we are in the summer," he says.

His diners used to spill out onto the sidewalk, waiting patently to get inside and eat. Then someone paid the restaurant the supreme compliment of opening a place two doors down with a very similar menu. The Sojourner just carried on in its usual style, gracious and mellow—but now you can get a table.

# SZECHWAN PEANUT PASTA

**10 ounces linguini**
**Peanut Sauce (recipe follows)**
**3 cups broccoli florets, steamed**
**1½ cups baby corn**
**3 cherry tomatoes, cut in half**
**1 cup sliced scallions**
**toasted sesame seeds for garnish**
**scallions for garnish**

Cook the linguini according to package directions, and toss it with the Peanut Sauce. Add the broccoli, tomatoes, baby corn, and scallions. Garnish with toasted sesame seeds and scallions, and serve immediately. Serves 6-8.

## Peanut Sauce

**1 cup roasted peanuts**
**1 cup vegetable stock**
**2 teaspoons soy sauce**
**¼ cup rice vinegar**
**¼ cup safflower oil**
**1 tablespoon sesame oil**
**2 tablespoons minced garlic**
**1½ teaspoons dry, crushed red pepper**

In a food processor, first grind the peanuts, then pour in the vegetable stock. Add the soy sauce, rice vinegar, safflower oil, sesame oil, garlic, and red pepper. Process until smooth. Makes about 2 cups.

# GYPSY LENTIL SOUP

¼ cup olive oil
1 1/3 cups chopped onion
2 teaspoons minced fresh garlic
2 green peppers, chopped
¾ cup diced celery
3 carrots, grated
8 cups vegetable stock
2 cups dried lentils, rinsed
¾ cup chopped dried apricots
2 2/3 cups canned tomatoes, chopped
½ teaspoon cinnamon
½ teaspoon allspice
½ teaspoon cayenne
1 teaspoon turmeric
1 tablespoon paprika
2 teaspoons salt
¼ cup chopped fresh parsley
2 tablespoons chopped fresh mint
fresh mint sprigs for garnish
sour cream for garnish

Using a 3½-quart saucepan, heat the oil. Add the onions, garlic, green peppers, celery, and carrots. Saute for approximately 10 minutes, then add the vegetable stock, rinsed lentils, and apricots. Bring to a boil, then reduce to a simmer and cover, cooking for approximately 45 minutes.

Add the tomatoes and dry spices, and continue to simmer, covered, for another 10 to 15 minutes. When the lentils are completely cooked, stir in the parsley and mint and serve. Garnish with a dollop of sour cream and 2 mint sprigs. Serves 6-8.

# TAHINI DRESSING

2/3 cup white vinegar
¼ cup lemon juice
½ cup water
½ tablespoon celery seed
1 tablespoon poppy seed
1 tablespoon Dijon mustard
¾ teaspoon salt
1 teaspoon granulated garlic
1 teaspoon oregano
1 teaspoon tarragon
1 teaspoon basil
¾ teaspoon onion powder
½ cup tahini
1 tablespoon honey
1 1/3 cups safflower oil

Blend the first 13 ingredients in a blender or food processor at low speed. Continue to blend while adding the honey and oil. Makes about 3½ cups. Can be used on salads, fish, or steamed vegetables.

# APPLE CRUNCH

5 pounds medium green apples
juice of ¼ lemon
¾ cup frozen unsweetened apple juice concentrate, thawed
¾ cup honey
1 tablespoon cinnamon
½ cup unbleached flour
½ cup raisins
Pastry Crust (recipe follows)
1 egg beaten with ½ teaspoon water
Topping (recipe follows)

Preheat the oven to 375 degrees. Peel, core, and slice the apples. Spread the apples in a large baking dish, and sprinkle with lemon juice. Mix the apples with the apple juice concentrate, honey, cinnamon, and ½ cup of flour. Bake the apples at 375 degrees for 20-30 minutes, stirring occasionally, until just tender. (The apples should be coated with a nice thick sauce.) Add the raisins and set aside.

Make the crust. Roll it out on a lightly floured surface, and line the bottom of a buttered, 9-inch x 13-inch baking dish with it. Trim the edges. Brush with egg wash. Prick with a fork. Bake the crust at 375 degrees for 10-15 minutes, until golden. Cool. Make the Topping.

Place the apples on top of the pre-baked crust. Cover with the Topping. Bake for 15-20 minutes at 375 degrees, until the topping is just lightly browned. Serve warm, or at room temperature. Serves 12.

## Pastry Crust

2¼ cups unbleached flour
1 teaspoon salt
½ cup butter
¼ cup vegetable shortening
½ cup cold milk

In a large bowl, sift the flour and salt together. Add the butter and vegetable shortening, cutting them in with a pastry blender until the mixture is crumbly. Sprinkle on the cold milk, and combine until the dough just holds together.

## Topping

1 teaspoon cinnamon
1¼ cups melted butter
½ cup honey
2 cups graham cracker crumbs
2 cups rolled oats
½ cup wheat germ
1½ cups chopped walnuts

Combine ingredients together in a large bowl.

# STONEHOUSE RESTAURANT

## Stonehouse Restaurant at the San Ysidro Ranch
## 900 San Ysidro Lane, Montecito
## 969-5046

For me, the style and simplicity of the San Ysidro Ranch represents true elegance. They don't have to flaunt a thing, because they have what really counts: history, lots of secluded acres, a wonderful view, and a kitchen that lives up to it all.

The restaurant, a white stone building that started out 150 years ago as a citrus packing plant for the Santa Barbara Mission, is the perfect setting for a civilized lunch, an elegant dinner, or a late morning, leisurely Sunday brunch. The atmosphere is relaxed, embellished at times with live piano music. Dress seems to vary from tennis clothes to taffeta, but somehow everyone looks his or her best. Through their constant vigilance, the staff leaves you free to concentrate on the delectable challenge of the meal, choosing from a selection of exquisitely prepared and beautifully presented foods.

When Claude Rouas, of L'Etoile in San Francisco and L'Auberge du Soleil in Napa, bought the San Ysidro Ranch in 1987, he didn't make drastic changes, although he simplified the decor. One of the most startling changes was probably changing the name from the Plow and Angel to Stonehouse. The public has forgiven this transgression, however, swayed by the wonderful food of chef Marc Ehrler. Claude Rouas had tried to get Marc for years, before finally succeeding. Marc says he's happy to be at the Ranch, because Santa

Barbara reminds him so much of the southeast of France, where he comes from.

Marc Ehrler says that Nouvelle Cuisine doesn't mean a thing to him. "My cooking is classical," he says. "I try not to mix more than three main ingredients; that's the most the palate can handle." Ehrler had the maintenance men build him his own smoker behind the kitchens, and he smokes his own fresh salmon for such specialties as the Smoked Salmon Tart with Salmon Caviar. He uses all local products, as fresh as he can get them. He was delighted to find Rond de Nice zucchini in Santa Barbara; they make the perfect bowls for the Lobster Soup in a Zucchini Bowl he shares here.

## *SMOKED SALMON TART WITH SALMON CAVIAR*

**4 circles of puff pastry, 4 inches in diameter and 1/8 inch thick (homemade or store bought)**
**½ cup heavy whipping cream**
**fresh lemon juice to taste**
**salt and pepper to taste**
**2 ounces salmon roe**
**2 tablespoons thinly chopped chives**
**12 ounces sliced smoked salmon**

Preheat the oven to 350 degrees. Place the 4 circles of puff pastry on a baking pan, with a rack on top of them to keep them from rising too high while baking. Bake at 350 degrees until dry, about 15-20 minutes. Remove from heat and keep at room temperature.

In a medium bowl, whip the cream until it is firm. Add the lemon juice, salt, and pepper to taste. Mix well. Add 1 ounce of the salmon roe and the chopped chives. Stir gently.

Spread a thin layer of the cream sauce over the puff pastry. Arrange the slices of salmon on top, giving it the look of a flower. Place on a plate, and spoon some sauce around the pastry. Sprinkle with the rest of the salmon roe. Serves 4 as an appetizer.

# LOBSTER SOUP IN A ZUCCHINI BOWL

**2 tablespoons olive oil**
**3 1-pound live lobsters**
**½ cup brandy**
**1 cup white wine**
**2 quarts water**
**2 stems fresh thyme**
**1 ounce bacon, diced**
**¼ cup carrots, diced**
**½ cup lentils**
**¼ cup tomatoes, diced**
**1 teaspoon saffron**
**4 Rond de Nice zucchini (a pale green, round zucchini)**

Heat the olive oil over high heat in a large saucepan, and add the lobsters. When they turn red, pour in the brandy. (Do not flambe.) Boil until the liquid is reduced to ¼, then add the white wine. Reduce this liquid to 2/3.

Take the lobsters out of the pan. Remove the meat from the shell, and set aside. Put the lobster shells back in the pan with the reduced wine. Add the water and thyme. Cook slowly for 30 minutes, then strain this stock.

Clean the pan, and cook the bacon slowly. Add the carrots, lentils, tomatoes, and saffron. Add the lobster stock. Cook for 30 minutes, until the lentils are soft.

Preheat the oven to 350 degrees. Cut off the tops of the zucchini, and reserve tops for lids. Scrape the pulp out of the zucchini. Put a little lobster meat into each zucchini, and pour the soup over it. Put the lids on, and place on a baking sheet. Bake at 350 degrees for 20 minutes, until hot. (This will also cook the zucchini.) Eat the soup, and then the bowl. Serves 4.

# VENISON WITH PASSION FRUIT SAUCE

2 tenderloins venison
2 cups red wine
2 ounces brandy
½ ounce vinegar
1 tablespoon olive oil
3 stems fresh thyme
2 cloves garlic
8 passion fruit, cut into chunks
3 tablespoons butter
salt and pepper to taste

Combine the red wine, brandy, vinegar, olive oil, thyme, and garlic in a dish large enough to hold the venison. Add the venison and marinate, covered, overnight in the refrigerator, turning occasionally.

The next day, remove the tenderloins from the marinade. Strain the marinade, and then place it over high heat, bring to a boil, and cook until reduced to 1/3. Add the passion fruit. Bring to a boil. Whip 1 tablespoon of the butter into this sauce, and add the salt and pepper. Remove from heat and keep warm.

Preheat the oven to 375 degrees. Saute the venison in 2 tablespoons of butter to brown it. Place in the oven, and roast until medium rare, about 10 minutes, or to desired preference. Slice the venison, arrange it on a plate, and pour the sauce over. Serves 4-6.

# HAZELNUT PARFAIT WITH COFFEE SAUCE

1 1/3 cups sugar
5 tablespoons water
½ cup egg yolks
½ cup ground hazelnuts, (or use praline, a French confection made from almonds and sugar)
1 teaspoon Frangelico liqueur
2 cups whipping cream
Coffee Sauce (recipe follows)

Cook the sugar and water together until it reaches 250 degrees on a candy thermometer. Place the yolks in a bowl, and beat with an electric mixer. As they blend, pour the sugar water mixture in slowly. The yolks will become whiter and lighter. Mix until cold, then add the hazelnuts (or praline) and liqueur.

Whip the cream until stiff. Fold into the mixture. Pour into 4 ramekins. Freeze for 4 hours.

Make the Coffee Sauce. Unmold the parfait and place them on 4 plates, with sauce all around. Serves 4.

## Coffee Sauce

6 egg yolks
2 cups milk
2/3 cup sugar
¼ cup fresh ground espresso beans

Beat the eggs yolks until frothy. In a separate saucepan, bring the milk and sugar to a boil. Pour the milk and sugar mixture over the eggs. Mix and put back in the saucepan. Cook over medium high heat, stirring with a wooden spoon, until the mixture is thick enough to coat the spoon. While still hot, add the ground espresso. Let the mixture infuse to taste (about 10 minutes), then strain the coffee grounds out. Makes about 3 cups.

## Tutti's
## 1209 Coast Village Road, Montecito
## 969-5800

With its turquoise, tiled pyramid tower and jaunty flags, Tutti's blew a breath of fresh air onto the Santa Barbara architecture scene a few years ago. Inside, tables are arranged around an open kitchen and deli area. The restaurant is festooned with hanging sausages, ropes of garlic and garlands of peppers, and a wonderful array of cheeses, wines, olive oils, vinegars and assorted sweets. Where the decor isn't hot pink and green, it's glass, chrome, and black marble. Very, very chic, and as charming as a wink.

The food is as good as the setting. Susan and Winston Sullivan have created a menu and an ambience that's all their own, a showcase for Susan's talented Italian cooking and Winston's low keyed finesse with the public. He even holds the babies, and they love it.

Winston said they named their restaurant Tutti's because they are open for breakfast, lunch and dinner and offer a little bit of everything, although they are basically an Italian restaurant. At breakfast you'll find their famous fried polenta as well as omelettes, cornbread French toast, and strawberry ricotta hotcakes.

Susan bakes all the breads and pastries, including the cheese flavored breadsticks and the Focaccia described here, a soft flat bread that has a loyal following of its own.

Susan's mother is from Verona and her father from Sicily, and the combination has produced a wonderful cuisine that seems to be constantly evolving. She says she likes to stay away from sophisticated northern Italian dishes, preferring "cuccina rustica" type food that can be easily made at home, like the Roasted Garlic and Onion recipes here. Her soups are imaginative and delicious, and her entrees include unique pasta, pizza, and chicken dishes, with fresh fish specials. Her recipe for the Canoe di Mele has a sentimental value for Susan; she got it from an 80-year-old cousin in Sicily.

# PASTA E CECI

½ cup extra virgin olive oil
1 cup chopped yellow onions
¼ cup minced fresh garlic
2 teaspoons minced fresh rosemary
1/8 teaspoon black pepper
2 cups cooked chick peas with their liquid
pinch of salt
4 cups chicken or vegetable stock
¼ pound diatini or other small soup pasta, cooked
freshly grated Parmesan cheese for garnish
extra virgin olive oil for garnish

Heat the olive oil over medium heat and saute the onions. Don't rush this step; onions should be a deep gold color. Add the garlic, rosemary, and pepper, and saute for another 10 minutes, stirring constantly. Do not allow garlic to burn. Add the chick peas with their liquid. Continue cooking and reduce liquid by ½. Add salt and chicken stock; bring to a boil. Remove from heat and puree all of the soup (or just half, depending on your preference). Return to the pan and re-heat. Add the pre-cooked pasta. To serve, sprinkle with Parmesan cheese and a drizzle of olive oil. Serves 4.

# FOCACCIO

¼ cup dry yeast
2 cups warm water
6-7 cups all purpose flour
2 teaspoons salt
½ cup extra virgin olive oil
1 cup water
Toppings (suggestions follow)

Dissolve the yeast in water, and let stand for 10 minutes. Pour 2 cups of the flour into a bowl, add the yeast mixture, and mix well. Cover and let stand for 30 minutes.

To this mixture, add the salt, olive oil, and 1 cup of water. Mix well. Add 2 cups of flour and mix well. Then add enough flour to make a fairly stiff dough. (Reserve 1 cup of flour to use for kneading.)

When you have a sufficiently stiff dough that can be easily handled during kneading, turn the dough out onto a work surface that has been dusted with flour. Kneed for 10 minutes, adding flour as necessary. When the dough is smooth, place it into a well-oiled bowl, cover it and let it double in size—about 1½ hours. (At this point the dough can be refrigerated overnight. Or divide it and bake half of it one day and half the next.)

Preheat the oven to 450 degrees. Cut the dough in half, and flatten it onto two well-oiled 10 x 15-inch cookie sheets. Allow the dough to rest again for 15 minutes. Stretch the dough into the corners of the pan. With your finger tips, make indentations all over the dough. Sprinkle a little olive oil over the top. Put on desired Topping and let rest for 10-15 minutes. If you have baking tiles, place the pans on the tiles. Bake at 450 degrees for 10-15 minutes. Serve immediately or remove from pan to a cooling rack so the bottom doesn't get soggy. Makes 20 5x3-inch slices.

# *Focaccio Toppings*

These can be basically anything you like. Begin with sea or kosher salt and coarsely ground pepper, and add any of the following:

**poppy or sesame seeds**
**fresh herbs, especially rosemary or sage**
**chopped green onions**
**chopped hash brown potatoes**
**Gorgonzola cheese and chopped tomatoes with a little fresh oregano**
**anchovy strips and cracked pepper**

# *CIPOLLI ARROSTI (ROASTED ONIONS)*

**8 yellow onions, preferably all the same size**
**¼ cup virgin olive oil**
**salt and fresh ground pepper**
**½ cup balsamic vinegar**
**grated Romano or Gorgonzola cheese (optional)**

Preheat oven to 250 degrees. Rub the unpeeled onions well with olive oil. Place them in a baking dish so they all fit snugly together. Sprinkle with salt and pepper. Bake at 250 degrees, uncovered, for about 1 to 1¼ hours. The onions should be soft to the touch but don't let them get too soft or mushy.

Remove from heat and set onions aside. Add the balsamic vinegar to the drippings in the pan, and put the pan on the stove. Heat, scraping the drippings and the vinegar together. Reduce until nicely thickened; remove from heat. Cut the onions in half or in quarters. If desired, sprinkle onions with grated Romano or Gorgonzola cheese, and place under the broiler to brown for a few minutes.

Pour the drippings over the onions and serve. Serve hot or at room temperature. Can be used on antipasto trays as snacks, or as a side dish. Serves 4.

# ROASTED GARLIC

**4 large firm, fresh heads garlic**
**extra virgin olive oil**
**sea salt and cracked black pepper to taste**

Preheat the oven to 250 degrees. Rub the garlic heads with olive oil, and set in a low sided roasting pan. Sprinkle with salt and black pepper. Bake for 2½ hours at 250 degrees. The garlic should feel soft when given a little squeeze.

Slice off the papery tops and serve warm. To eat, break cloves apart and push the garlic pulp out. It can be spread on bread as an appetizer, or served with grilled meat as a side dish. Serves 4.

# *CANOE DI MELE (SICILIAN BAKED APPLES)*

1 cup granulated sugar
½ cup dark brown sugar
1 teaspoon cinnamon
½ teaspoon allspice
½ teaspoon nutmeg
1 pound filo dough
½ pound melted butter
1 cup currants tossed with ¼ cup Meyers dark rum
9 Granny Smith apples, peeled, cored, and cut in half
1 cup toasted almonds
powdered sugar for garnish

In a small bowl, mix the sugars and spices together. Cut the sheets of filo dough in half crosswise. Take one sheet of filo and brush it lightly with butter. Sprinkle a little sugar and cinnamon mixture over it. Repeat until you have 36 pieces of buttered, sugared, filo dough. Take the dough and make 9 stacks of 4 layers each. In the center of each stack, make a mound of 1/9th of the currants and place 2 apple halves, core side down, but overlapping slightly, on the currants. Brush the apples with butter, dust with cinnamon mixture, and top with 1/9th the toasted almonds. Repeat until you have 9 canoe.

Fold the 4 sheets of filo up and around the apples of each canoe. Tuck the ends under neatly. The apples should poke up through the top of the filo slightly. Brush again with butter. (At this point they will keep in the refrigerator for up to a week.) Preheat oven to 375 degrees. Place on a baking sheet and bake at 375 degrees for about 20 minutes. (The dough should be golden brown and the apples just barely firm.) Dust with powdered sugar. Serves 9, or 18 if cut in half.

# WINE CASK

## The Wine Cask
## 813 Anacapa Street, Santa Barbara
## 966-9463

In 1872, brothers Doug and Hugh Margerum took over the wine store in El Paseo. Although they retained the name, the Wine Cask, their business has evolved to the point where the name conjures up good food as quickly as it does good wine. Doug Margerum was 21 at the time; Hugh was 26. This may account for the energy behind the growth, the constant surprises, and the numerous special events the restaurant offers.

Originally they built a tasting bar adjacent to the wine shop, based on the concept of an English wine bar. Soon they were serving soups and appetizers, and the demand for more food just kept growing. In 1985 they added a small, well-equipped kitchen and brought in a chef; and a year later they began their catering business, run by Doug's wife, Laurel.

The restaurant has an intimate dining room with a handsome wine bar that allows customers of the wine shop to do some tasting. Diners can also wander into the store and select their own wine to be served with a $4 corkage fee. Cloth-covered tables lit by low hanging lamps give the atmosphere of a civilized private club. Tables have also been set up outside on the old flagstones of the back patio of historic El Paseo. But the friendly, caring service and the savory food are the main ingredients of a memorable encounter with this restaurant.

Chef Tom Hansen maintains the Wine Cask's reputation as one of the finest and most imaginative restaurants in Santa Barbara. His inventive, nouvelle cuisine menu, featuring fresh seafood, pasta and meat dishes, changes every two weeks.

The desserts alone are worth a visit to the restaurant. Hansen says that he has been doing a lot of Southwestern dishes lately. He made a cactus tequila sauce for a pheasant dish, and he liked it so much he decided to try it as a sorbet. The result is his recipe here for Cactus Pear Tequila Sorbet with Tangerine Lime Sauce.

# WARM SCALLOP MOUSSE WITH MANGO MELON LIME SAUCE

**3 ounces boneless whitefish (sole, halibut, etc.)**
**12 ounces scallops**
**1 egg white**
**1 cup heavy cream**
**salt and white pepper to taste**
**Mango Melon Lime Sauce (recipe follows)**

Grind the whitefish in a food grinder (or have your fish monger grind it), and chill. In a food processor, process the scallops briefly. Add the whitefish, and process for 10-15 seconds. Add the egg white, and process for another 10-15 seconds. Slowly add the heavy cream in a steady stream. Puree it until somewhat smooth (20 to 30 seconds). Chill for 15 minutes. Pass the mixture through a fine sieve and season with salt and pepper. (Additional cream may be needed, around ¼-½ cup. To test, poach a little of the mixture in boiling water to see if it becomes firm.)

Preheat the oven to 300 degrees. Butter or spray 6 ramekins, and fill with the fish. Place the ramekins in a shallow pan with 1 inch of water and bake at 300 degrees until set, about 15-20 minutes.

Make the Lime Sauce. Place a little sauce on a plate, remove the mousse from the baking dishes, and place on the sauce. Serves 6.

# Mango Melon Lime Sauce

½ cup sliced shallots
1 cup port
½ cup white wine vinegar
½ cup white wine
¼ cup heavy cream
½-¾ cup sweet butter, cut in little pieces
¼ cup diced mango
¼ cup diced papaya
¼ cup diced cantaloupe or honeydew
juice of 1 lime

In a saute pan, cook the shallots, port, and vinegar until all the liquid has evaporated. Add the wine and cream, and bring to a boil. Boil until liquid is reduced by half. Lower heat and slowly add the butter, piece by piece, and whisk until it has formed a thick sauce. Strain the sauce. Add the fruit and lime juice. Makes about 2 cups sauce.

# GRILLED SWORDFISH
# WITH TAMARILLO PAPAYA SALSA

Tamarillo Papaya Salsa (recipe follows)
½ cup olive oil
3 cloves garlic, chopped
3 shallots, chopped
¼ cup cilantro, chopped plus a few sprigs for garnish
2 limes, zest and juice
6 swordfish steaks, 6 ounces each
papaya slices for garnish

Make the Tamarillo Papaya Salsa according to directions.

Combine the oil, garlic, shallots, cilantro, lime zest, and lime juice in a dish large enough to hold the fish. Marinate the fish in the lime-oil mixture for ½ hour before cooking, turning once.

Prepare the grill and cook the steaks for 3-4 minutes on each side, making criss-cross patterns on the steaks, and basting them with the marinade while cooking. Place the Salsa on 6 plates, and place the steaks on top. Garnish with cilantro and slices of papaya. Serves 6.

## *Tamarillo Papaya Salsa*

**3-4 tamarillos, skinned and diced**
**½ papaya, skinned, seeded, and diced**
**½ small red bell pepper, diced**
**½ small yellow bell pepper, diced**
**2 large shallots, minced**
**1-2 jalapenos, seeded and minced**
**¼ cup chopped cilantro leaves**
**juice of 1 lime**
**1 tablespoon rice wine vinegar**
**salt to taste**

Put all the ingredients together in a bowl and mix well. Set aside, or refrigerate for at least 1 hour to allow the flavors to infuse. Makes about 2 cups.

# ROASTED LOIN OF VENISON WITH HUCKLEBERRY CHIPOTLE SAUCE

**½ large carrot, diced**
**½ large celery stick, diced**
**½ large onion, chopped**
**1 sprig each of rosemary, savory, and thyme**
**1 bay leaf**
**6 peppercorns**
**1 cup red wine**
**¼ cup olive oil**
**2 cloves garlic, chopped**
**2 pounds 4 ounces venison loin (saddle)**
**Huckleberry Chipotle Sauce (recipe follows)**
**1 ounce clarified butter**

In a medium saucepan, combine the carrot, celery, onion, rosemary, savory, thyme, bay leaf, peppercorns, and red wine. Bring to a boil over high heat, then lower heat and simmer 10-15 minutes. Add the olive oil and cool.

Cut the venison into 6 6-ounce portions. Place them in a container with the vegetable-wine mixture and marinate, covered, for 24-72 hours. Turn occasionally.

Preheat the oven to 500 degrees. Make the Huckleberry-Chipotle Sauce and set aside. Put the clarified butter in a skillet on a high flame. When the butter is melted, add the venison and sear on both sides. Place in a baking dish, and roast in the oven at 500 degrees for 6-9 minutes (depending on desired doneness). Let rest for 4-5 minutes. Slice. Put the sauce on a serving plate, and arrange slices of meat on top. Serves 6.

## *Huckleberry Chipotle Sauce*

½-1 chipotle chili (available at Mexican markets)
1 teaspoon clarified butter or oil
4 shallots, sliced
1 cup huckleberries
½ cup port
1-1¼ cups veal demi-glace (stock which has been reduced to a
    syrup thick enough to coat the back of a spoon)
2-4 tablespoons sweet butter
salt to taste

Seed the chipotle and dice it. In a saucepan, put the clarified butter or oil over medium high heat. When hot, add the chili, and saute for 15-30 seconds. Add the shallots and saute for another 15-30 seconds. Add the berries and port. Bring to a boil and boil until liquid is reduced by half. Add enough demi-glace to get a nice sauce consistency. Puree, strain through a chinois, and stir in the sweet butter. Keep warm until ready to serve. Makes about 1 cup.

# CACTUS PEAR TEQUILA SORBET WITH TANGERINE LIME SAUCE

1½ cups sugar
1 cup water
12-16 cactus pears
¼ cup clear tequila
2 egg whites (optional)
Tangerine Lime Sauce (recipe follows)

Place the sugar and water in a saucepan, and boil until the sugar is dissolved. Cool and refrigerate.

Cut the ends off the cactus pears, and then make a slit lengthwise on the fruit. The peel will come off very easily. Puree the pears in a food processor, and strain the mixture through a fine sieve. (You should have 2 cups.) Add the tequila and egg whites (if using), and freeze in an ice cream maker according to manufacturer's directions. Make the Tangerine Lime Sauce, and serve the sorbet with the sauce. Makes 1 quart.

## Tangerine Lime Sauce

1½ cups tangerine juice
¼ cup sugar
juice of 1-2 limes

In a small saucepan, mix the tangerine juice with the sugar, and boil until only ½ cup of the liquid remains. Add the lime juice and chill. Makes about 1 cup.

## Zelo
### 630 State Street, Santa Barbara
### 966-5792

Zelo is such a hip place, it seems more like a Los Angeles or New York restaurant. It's a long, lean space, with a big brick wall that displays great art, and there's always a large, spectacular floral arrangement near the door.

The open kitchen is along one wall towards the front of the restaurant, with a generous wine bar beyond it. On the other side, beneath the warm glow cast by tiny colored lights, the tables are arranged on lots of different levels, making the atmosphere very intimate. I like the stream-lined 40's style booths right in the windows on State Street.

Bob Stout, who owns Zelo, was one of the partners who started the Sojourner, so his credentials for healthy, wholesome food are impeccable. Zelo is more upscale, however, and the menu is sophisticated and innovative. This restaurant reveres vegetables and salads and does them very well; and there's a number of vegetarian entrees every day, like pasta primavera, as well as chicken and fresh fish.

Chef Jennifer Maloney came to Zelo from the Wine Cask, where she had been the sous chef. She's an adventurous cook who's not afraid of experimenting with unusual flavors. She makes delicious gourmet pizza, like Pesto Chicken Calzone, and what she calls "Big Food," entrees like Mustard Chicken Fettuccine. No one in town makes a nacho nibble quite like Zelo's Fried Sweet Potato Chips featured here—sweet, spicy, and hard to stop eating once you get hold of a hot basketful. It comes with a wonderful Banana Curry dipping sauce too.

After a mellow evening of dining pleasure, at around 10 o'clock, Zelo turns into a very popular dance club. It adds a certain electricity to the place.

# *ROASTED EGGPLANT AND GARLIC SOUP*

**4 large, firm eggplant**
**3 tablespoons olive oil**
**salt and pepper to taste**
**1 onion, diced**
**1 head of garlic, peeled**
**1 red pepper, diced**
**4 ripe tomatoes**
**1 teaspoon oregano**
**1 teaspoon rosemary**
**1 quart water or chicken stock**
**1 cup cream**
**roasted peppers for garnish**
**grated Parmesan cheese for garnish**

Rub the eggplant with a little of the olive oil, sprinkle with salt and pepper, and roast them in a 375 degree oven for 40 minutes. Remove from the oven, cool, and cut into small pieces.

In a large skillet, heat the remaining oil over medium high heat, and saute the eggplant with the onions, garlic, peppers, tomatoes, and herbs. Add the water or stock, and season with salt and pepper to taste. Bring to a boil, then lower heat and simmer for 45 minutes. Puree in a blender. Return to the pot, add the cream, and heat gently until hot but not boiling. Garnish with roasted peppers and Parmesan cheese. Serves 6.

# SPICY FRIED SWEET POTATOES WITH BANANA CURRY DIPPING SAUCE

**Banana Curry Sauce (recipe follows)**
**4 sweet potatoes, peeled, washed and sliced thin**
**cayenne powder to taste**
**thyme to taste**
**salt and pepper to taste**

Make the Curry Sauce according to directions. Fry the potatoes until crisp using any standard French fry recipe. Sprinkle with cayenne, thyme, salt, and pepper. Serve warm, with Banana Curry Sauce on the side. Serves 6.

## Banana Curry Sauce

**1½ cups cream or coconut milk**
**2 tablespoons curry powder**
**2 tablespoons honey**
**1 ripe banana**
**1 teaspoon coconut**

Mix ingredients together. Makes about 1½ cups.

# LEMON CUSTARD TART
# WITH BLUEBERRIES

1 cup flour
5 ounces butter
¼ cup sugar
2 egg yolks
2 tablespoons cold water
1 cup heavy cream
¾ cup sugar
7 whole eggs
juice and zest of 6 lemons
1 cup blueberries
powdered sugar for garnish

Put the flour in a food processor. Slowly add the butter, sugar, egg yolks, and water. When the dough starts to form a ball, stop the machine. Scrape out the dough, wrap it in plastic, and chill for 1 hour.

Preheat the oven to 375 degrees. Roll out the pastry dough and place it on a 10-inch tart pan. Chill for 10 minutes. Bake the shell until half done at 375 degrees, approximately 10 minutes.

Meanwhile, make the filling by combining the cream, sugar, eggs, lemons and blueberries in a large bowl. Stir well. Remove tart shell from the oven, add the filling, and cook for 45 minutes at 375 degrees, until firm. Dust with powdered sugar before serving. Serves 6-8.

# *Index*

## Fish (see Seafood)

## Lamb
Broiled Lamb Loin with Roasted Garlic and Oyster Mushroom and
  Green Peppercorn Sauce, 163
Couscous Royal, 32
Hunter's Lamb, 82
Lamb Shanks with Tomatillo and Cilantro Sauce, 129
Roasted Lamb Loin with Fresh Herbs, 113

## Pancakes
Blue and Golden Corn Cakes, 114
Crepes, 48
Goat Cheese Pancakes, 104
Potato Pancakes, 112

## Pasta
Capellini al Pomodoro Naturale (Angel Hair Pasta with Fresh Tomato
  and Basil), 132
Fettuccine Colombo, 49
Fettuccine Santa Barbara, 82
Pasta e Ceci, 185
Roma Ravioli, 19
Seafood Pad Thai (Seafood Noodles), 166
Szechwan Pasta, 152
Szechwan Peanut Pasta, 175
Tomato Linguini with Chicken and Ginger, 24
Veal Lasagne, 50

## Pizza
Pizza with Caramelized Onions and Gorgonzola Cheese, 96

## Pork
Braised Pork Loin with Cider/Sage Sauce, 64
Cajun Shepherd Pie, 39
Godzilla's Gyosa, 85
Paella a la Catalana, 77
Pot Stickers, 76

## Poultry
Blackened Chicken with Pecan Butter Sauce, 162
Chiang's Duck with Garlic Sauce, 54
Chicken Fricassee, 125
Chicken in Mole Poblano Sauce, 37

**Rabbit**

**Relishes**

**Rice**

## Salads

## Salsa (see Relishes)

## Sauces

## Seafood

## Side Dishes

## Soups

## Tacos and Tortilla Dishes

## Veal